HELP! I'M A MUM

Finding wisdom for raising children as disciples of Jesus

Lexia G Mackin

ELGEM BOOKS

Copyright ©2019, Lexia G Mackin

All rights reserved. No part of this publication may be reproduced, stored in a retrieval system, or transmitted in any form or by any means, electronic, mechanical, photocopying, recording, or otherwise, without the prior written permission of the publisher. All rights reserved. No part of this publication may be reproduced, distributed, or transmitted in any form or by any means, including photocopying, recording, or other electronic or mechanical methods, without the prior written permission of the publisher, except in the case of brief quotations embodied in reviews and certain other non-commercial uses permitted by copyright law.

ISBN: 978-0-9757679-1-7

Dedication

I would like to dedicate this book to the following people, all of whom have contributed in some way to its writing:

My husband
You have always encouraged me to press on and to achieve my best. Your faith in my ability has never diminished. You have been a faithful husband and partner in the walk of the Kingdom. Thank you.

My children
You have been with us both in the good times and in the bad. You have chosen to love us, even though we weren't perfect. Thank you.

My foster children
You have taught me much about parenting with a different heart. You chose to love not just us but our whole family, and to become part of it. Thank you.

My family in Jesus
You prophetically called me "a mother in Israel". You have given me many women who have contributed to my knowledge and experience. You shared my fear and, like me, were too scared to leave hospital with your first born, for fear of failure or inadequacy. Thank you.

Contents

Introduction 7

What is Discipleship? 13
   Making Disciples 13
   Discipleship in Action 15
   Characteristics of a Disciple 16
   Education vs Training 24
   Correction, Discipline, Punishment and Reward 26

Stepping Stones to Maturity 35
   Birth-4 months 36
   4-8 months 37
   8-12 months 39
   1-2 years 41
   2-5 years 44

Boundaries, Choice and Consequence 51
   Choice and Consequence 51
   What are Boundaries? 57
   Family Roles and Responsibilities 61
   Parenting Styles 72
   Clear Communications 74

Correcting Inappropriate Behaviour............79

The Role of Parents in Setting Standards 79

Training in Righteousness.. 82

Correction in Training 86

The Purpose of Correction 86

In the Prayer Closet 89

Beyond Foundations 97

Foundations 97

Foundations of the Faith 111

Teaching Foundations 114

Introduction

Titus 2:4-5a *"...so the younger women will be loving wives and mothers. Each of the younger women must be sensible and kind, as well as good homemakers, who puts her husband first," CEV*

This job has never been done before—you are the first! There are plenty of mothers who have raised their own children—each with their individual experiences, mistakes and advice—but no-one has ever parented *your* particular child. Even when we have had experience with our first child, our second child will be totally different. Each time we have a child, we begin again at the beginning.

This book provides practical tips, examples from real life experiences, and Biblical principles on discipleship. This is a journey—so buckle up and hang on!

Another book on child-rearing. Really? What expertise do I bring? Let me say up-front: I'm not a psychologist or any other sort of academic. This is a series of practical topics to help you along the way and to help you establish a direction in your training. "From the kitchen table", you might say—from someone who has already made most of the mistakes that can be made in child-rearing, but who has learned along the way.

"Why do I need a direction?" I hear you say. "Isn't being mum just about doing the chores, driving the kids to their sports and dance activities, and generally punishing for bad behaviour?" If that's what you think about being a mum, you're at least one step ahead of where I was as a new mum. I didn't have a clue! It wasn't something I thought about at all. It just happened. In fact, I was well on the way to a promising business career as a Change

Management trainer/coach. I had determined to not get married. Men were only after one thing (at least the ones I dated) and I was jaded, to say the least.

Then I had a life-changing moment where I came into relationship with the God of creation. I began reading my Bible and discovered that when God created something *"it was good"* (Genesis 1:4). Did that apply to the male gender of our species as well?

Instinctively, of course, I knew it did; but still needed a few weeks to process what I had discovered and how it applied to me. I could generally accept that what He made was *"good"*, but I baulked a little at the concept that males were also created *"good"*-based on my previous experience.

So, I prayed and asked God if He would show me one male that was good. That's all I wanted: just one. I didn't ask for a husband. I didn't ask for a boyfriend. I just wanted to see one male that demonstrated God's goodness. I didn't know, at the time, that God is able to do *"exceedingly abundantly above all that we ask or think"* (Ephesians 3:20 KJV).

You guessed it! I got a husband.

Personal Uncertainty

Now, I had to change my thinking. I needed to include the idea of a "husband" in my life. I came to the place where I accepted that. After all, it wasn't that hard, because this was a man who definitely showed me the goodness of God.

The direction of my life changed as I relented. "OK, God. I'll get married, but I definitely won't have children!" Well, five children later, you can see that I have had a quantum-leap mind shift—and God is still quite chuffed at how He ambushed my life!

You might be tempted to think that, with a background as a Change Management trainer/coach, I was fully capable of training my own children right from the start. Wrong! I was an only child who grew up in a boarding school. What did I know about babies? In fact, when it was time to go home from the hospital with my first bundle of joy, I decided to ask a nurse if I could stay in the hospital "for just one day longer". Alas, when I finally found a nurse, my throat was so constricted by fear that I couldn't get the words out!

I survived my first baby and, more importantly, he survived me! I was madly in love; our little family was growing, and life was good. What could possibly go wrong? If we loved each other enough, and if we loved our children, surely life would be wonderful. Right?

Wrong! By the time we had three children, all twenty-two months apart (unplanned, I assure you), our church affiliation was with a home-based, "shepherding movement".

Social Uncertainty

In the 1970s, there was a major social upheaval. We were beginning to ask who we were as a nation. The "White Australia Policy" was being scrapped; we were withdrawing from a war in Vietnam that we didn't really understand; the role of women (particularly) in the workforce, as it related to "equal work, equal pay", was being examined; Indigenous Australians were making waves with land rights; and the infamous dismissal of a sitting Prime Minister rocked the nation.

That Prime Minister, of course, was Gough Whitlam, the one who had major reforms in Education, the Family Law Court, Foreign Affairs, Indigenous Australian policy, Health and Industrial Affairs.

We were still living in the "hippie" culture of the 1960s, but the fringe element of the left-wing environmental movement was gaining traction and becoming more mainstream, largely due to the Arab nations' decision to stop supplying oil to the west in protest over America's support for Israel. Public anxiety was increasing, and we didn't know how to stop it. And that was just the secular world.

The church culture was no better! A famous televangelist and Assemblies of God minister, James Orsen Bakker, became infamous with the alleged rape of his secretary and the cover-up of hush money. Subsequent uncovering of accounting fraud led to a conviction with imprisonment and a divorce from his wife, Tammy. In 1980, he wrote a book, "Eight Keys to Success" in which he stated, *"God wants you to be happy, God wants you to be rich, God wants you to prosper"*. This typified the emerging excesses of a part of the church scene and left ordinary Christians reeling, not knowing which way to turn.

Shepherding Movement

Then, there emerged an alternative in the form of the "shepherding movement". It promulgated a lifestyle of obedience and sacrifice; of submission to a "shepherd"; of purity and righteousness not evidenced in the current secular or church culture.

We were IN! We wanted an alternative lifestyle to what we saw as the problems of our day and we saw it in the movement. What we didn't know at the time, was that the basic foundation for this movement was built on shaky ground. However, this book is not so much about the issues of the "shepherding movement" as it is about the fact that, as new parents, we needed help, and this was our source of help.

We were taught by our "shepherd" how to bring up our children "in obedience"—but I later learned, be revelation, that *obedience without love is legalism;* that *correction without mercy and grace is criticism.* So, with the best of intentions, and the worst advice in the world, we embarked on raising a family of five children.

Discipleship in the Home

After having five children of my own, I was privileged to foster two more girls. They had been placed in foster care because of family drug addiction and neglect. Suddenly, I was bound by the laws of Australia. I couldn't train them as I had my own children—which may have been a good thing—and I was now accountable to government representatives for the outcome of my parenting.

This caused me to have a major rethink of all I had been taught. It was a wonderful opportunity for me to delve into discipleship in the home.

Although I had previously considered myself a disciple of Jesus at my conversion, I thought this was a personal decision, a personal relationship. It wasn't until much later in my walk with Him that I understood His injunction to *"make disciples"*. Although I had thought of myself as a disciple, I didn't really have anyone bringing me into a mature relationship with Jesus so that I could reap the benefits of discipleship.

This has been a fairly recent revelation. So, the information in this book is about my journey of *"making disciples"* in the family context—not just another book on child-rearing.

What is Discipleship?

Luke 6:40 *"A disciple is not above his teacher, but everyone who is perfectly trained will be like his teacher."*

In this chapter we will cover…

- Biblical discipleship
- The difference between education, training, and discipleship
- Seven characteristics of a disciple
- The difference between correction, discipline, and punishment
- The training event
- The importance of reward

Making Disciples

Jesus told us in ***Matthew 28:19-20*** (LITV), *"Then having gone, disciple all nations, baptising them into the name of the Father and of the Son and of the Holy Spirit, teaching them to observe all things, whatever I commanded you. And, behold, I am with you all the days until the completion of the age. Amen."*

These verses have sometimes been referred to—by people who are much more scholarly than I am—as imperative. That simply means it is a command; we don't have a choice about whether we want to be obedient to Jesus. There is also an inherent order of completion:

In your going: We are to be active in our obedience to the command of Jesus in all of our comings and goings, i.e. in our daily life. We don't have to be "missionaries" as such, but as we go to work, to the supermarket, to school, to sport and dance, we are going.

Disciple all nations: We shouldn't just tell, educate, or even train. We should use the discipleship model that Jesus used. We shouldn't just stick with our own ethnic group but be open to any group that our Father places in our way.

Baptise: This is into the Name. There is only one Name, and it is the name of Jesus—the same name (or character) of the Father and the Spirit. This may be a contentious issue, depending on which denomination we belong to, but the Bible is simple: it says, "into the Name". There is only one name. Notice also that baptism comes before teaching!

Teach: The goal of teaching Jesus' way is *observation of all things*. By implication, it is all the things that Jesus taught concerning the Kingdom of God.

I am with you: We don't do this on our own; Jesus, by the Spirit, is ALWAYS with us.

Discipleship in Action

It may be helpful for us to see discipleship in action and the best place to see this, of course, is in the gospels as each of the writers tell us something of the process that Jesus used with His twelve.

If we begin our gospel search at Matthew and work our way through each of the gospels, it may take a while and we may miss something that is fundamental to our understanding of discipleship, so we'll jump straight into the gospel of John.

Notice what Jesus says in John 17:4: "*…I have finished the work that you gave me to do.*" For many of my Christian years, I didn't ask myself what work He was talking about. I assumed He was talking about the work of salvation as that was my only understanding of the purpose of Jesus in coming to this earth. When I looked a little closer, I saw that Jesus said twice that He had finished the work. In John 19:30, He says *"It is finished"* when He gave up His Spirit and died. That was His work of salvation—when He died for our sins.

So, what work had He finished in John 17:4? Was He just repeating Himself? No. The context of Chapter 17 tells me it was no idle repetition. If we follow His train of thought, we see that Jesus was saying He had demonstrated the Father's glory (v4); He had finished the work (v4); He had manifested or revealed the name (the character) of the Father to the men that the Father had given Him (v6). These men had kept the Father's word.

Here is the essence of Jesus' discipleship. He had revealed the nature of the Father to the twelve men, given to Him by the Father. The old adage says it simply: *like father, like son*. We look and act in the same way as the one who has fathered us.

How did Jesus conduct His discipleship? Matthew 4:17 says that Jesus *"began to preach and to say, 'Repent! For the kingdom of Heaven has drawn near'"* (LITV). Then, in verses 18-22, we see Jesus calling His disciples. That shows that the disciples knew what they were getting in to. Jesus could see that they had a heart for the things of the Father and were willing to learn the ways of this new kingdom that Jesus was ushering into the world.

Characteristics of a Disciple

Dwell in His Word

Anyone can disciple someone! You can be a Buddhist and have disciples; You can be an artist and have disciples. This book is specifically about being a disciple of Jesus from a parenting perspective.

John 8:31 tells us that we are His disciples if we *"abide in His word"*. We need to be dwelling in His word, reading it daily, putting in to practice the principles and instructions we read. A disciple is *one who believes what he reads, not one who reads what he already believes!*

Bear Fruit

This abiding process will bear fruit! When the storms of life surround us—as they surely will at some stage in our lives—we will be grounded in Jesus and the power of His word, bearing fruit that remains through having answered prayer (John 15:16).

Be Obedient

One of the things I like about reading the gospel of Mark, is his use of the word *"immediately"*. In Mark 1:16, Jesus called Simon and Andrew, then in verse 18, "they immediately followed Him"; the same with James and John. Again, in chapter 2, *"immediately many gathered together"* to hear Him preach (NKJ). The disciples saw Jesus preach, heal, and deliver. So, we see that one of the characteristics of a disciple is obedience that is quick to respond to the command.

Love

Another thing that Jesus demonstrated with His disciples was loving and serving. He said, "*...as I have loved you, you should also love one another*" in John 13:34. He demonstrated that love, and then instructed them to love others according to His demonstration. It wasn't just a 30-minute sermon on the 7 Best Ways to Demonstrate Love. It was love in action!

Love is the one characteristic that will tell those around us whose disciples we are (John 13:35). Remember, we can be disciples to anyone. But I'm presuming you're reading this book because you love Jesus and want to follow His ways, walk in His Spirit and reflect Him on this earth. That means that we can be a *"partaker of the divine nature"*—adding the divine nature of Jesus, Himself—to our faith (2 Peter 1:4-5 LITV).

Do the Work of the Master

In Luke 9, we read how Jesus sent out His twelve to do the works that He was sent to do—**P**reach, **H**eal and **D**eliver (the PHD of the Kingdom of God!). The plan, coming from verse 1, was that they were given both power and authority over all demons and to heal the sick. Verse six then tells us that they went out preaching and healing. The **PHD**s of the Kingdom of God were all covered. So, another thing we see is that a disciple does the work of the Master.

Report Back

In Luke 10, Jesus then sent out seventy disciples. Verse 9 tells us the instructions were the same. They were to **H**eal and **P**reach the Kingdom of God. When they returned, in verse 17, they reported back to Jesus on their mission. **Reporting back** is another characteristic of a disciple. They also were joyful that *"even the demons were subject to us through Your Name"* (LITV). Again, they did the PHDs of the Kingdom of God.

Receive Correction

They did the same work that the Father had given Jesus to do. They, also, were overjoyed at the response of their ministry but notice that, in verse 20, Jesus gives them correction. He says not to be overjoyed at their ministry but to *"rejoice that your names are written in heaven"* (LITV). Another characteristic of a disciple is that they are **corrected** by their Master.

For more information on Discipleship, I recommend a website: www.revivalministries.org.au. This website has an immense array of free training materials for those who want to follow discipleship more purposefully.

But now we need to ask ourselves, "How does education and training affect discipleship?" Is there a difference between them or are they just saying the same thing?

Education

In Jesus' day, there were two models of teaching. One was the Greek method and the other was the Hebrew, or Jewish, method. Greek education was mostly formal and was primarily for males. It was provided in a public-school setting, much like our schools today, and included both intellectual and physical disciplines. The Romans followed this style of education, progressing from an informal familial style to a tuition-based system provided by private tutors.

Early Roman education was based on the Classical Greek tradition where only children of the rich were educated, mostly by private tutors, in the home. Those who couldn't afford private tutors sent their children to a private school. These schools were often attached to a marketplace stall. The children would rise very early in the morning and stay until it was time for dinner and bedtime at home—very long day for a child of any age!

There were two main types of schools: the first type of school was for younger children who were taught to read and write and do basic mathematics. They practiced their writing with a stylus and wax tablet, and it wasn't until they were older, and more competent, that they were allowed to use paper made from papyrus. Both girls and boys went to this school up to the age of around 11 or 12, but only if their parents could afford the tuition. During lessons, if they answered incorrectly, the teacher would beat them with a cane.

The second type of school was mostly for older males. They would study specific topics to prepare them for life in society, such as public speaking and philosophy. Girls, particularly those from rich families, received an education in the home. They were taught how to run a good household and how to be a good wife, in general. Their subjects included things like music, sewing, and running a kitchen.

> "The teacher must decide how to deal with his pupil. Some boys are lazy, unless forced to work; others do not like being controlled; some will respond to fear but others are paralysed by it. Give me a boy who is encouraged by praise, delighted by success and ready to weep over failure. Such a boy must be encouraged by appeals to his ambitions."

This was said by Quintilian, a teacher in the 1st Century AD.

Greek and Roman education was primarily concerned with informing the mind and training the body; Jewish education was for the purpose of worshiping God.

Hebrew Education

Although the Hebrews did have public schools, originating from Ezra (459 BCE), these schools were for fatherless boys from the age of 16 and upwards. The schools filled a social gap for families without fathers and were conducted in the "house of the teacher". Girls did not attend these schools, but they were expected to read and write, participate in commerce as an independent woman, and educate their own children before the age of seven.

Abraham is recorded, in Genesis 18:19, as one who commanded his children and his household after him, to *"keep the way of Jehovah, to do righteousness and justice"* (LITV). Under Moses, the children of Israel were instructed to teach their children all the statutes (or laws) spoken by Yahweh (Leviticus 10:11). More specific instructions were given in Deuteronomy 6:7; *"Teach them to your sons, and shall speak of them as you sit in your house, and as you walk in the way, and as you are lying down, and as you are rising up"* (LITV). In other words, in the home, all the time!

The main purpose of this instruction was to know the Torah (literally *Instruction or Teaching*) so that their children knew how to worship God. Most of this instruction was given by the mother, as well as instruction in morals, faith, and values.

Schools were introduced into Jewish culture by Joshua ben Gamia (64 CE) where they learned the *Mikra* (written Torah, the first five books of the Bible) at 5-6 years of age, *Mishnah* (Torah, or oral traditions) at ten, fulfilled *Mitzvoth* (moral kindnesses over and above the law) at thirteen, and the *Talmud* (comprehension and contemplation of Torah) at fifteen. Before these formal schools, the mother would have taught reading, writing, and the Mikra.

So, we can see that, although schools did exist in early Jewish society, education really began in the home for children, primarily facilitated by the mother, even before the age of five or six. When this education was completed, boys were then ready to go with their father and learn the family business. Joseph was a carpenter, so Jesus learned how to be a carpenter. It wasn't just the technical skills; it was also about who to offer credit to, who was honest and trustworthy, and so on.

Jesus' comments, in Luke 2:49 where He says *"Why did you look for me? Did you not know that I must be busy in the affairs of My Father?"* (LITV) can now be put into the context of His overall mission on earth. He had finished with His mother's education and was now ready to learn His Father's business—and He wasn't talking about Joseph. He was talking about His Father in heaven, saying that He must now learn the business of the Kingdom of God!

Today's Schools

Today's schools are still based on the same Greek model—that of having a cohort of children in the one class where formal studies on any number of subjects is undertaken. Thankfully, there are teachers with a good heart who seek the welfare of the child in their teaching. Most schools also offer a wider variety of subjects and students have a choice in which subjects they want to master.

In the western world, we are fortunate enough to have the choice between sending our children to a school or keeping them at home for "home schooling" or "distance education". In this book, I am not advocating for one method of formal schooling over another. What I do want to explain is how we can disciple our children to Jesus, in the home, for however long we have them. The best and most productive method of discipling is training.

The School Jesus Used

Jesus chose twelve men to be His disciples (Luke 6:12-13) after He spent all night in prayer. These disciples (learners, pupils) spent all their time with Him. He was the Teacher, the Master. Matthew 4:20 tells us they left their boats, their livelihoods, to follow Him. This shows us that true discipleship is not just a training or education program; it is not about going to a conference and learning the principles of discipleship; it isn't even about having a mentor. **True discipleship is a lifestyle** where the principles are lived out in daily, real-life situations. That's why the best place to learn discipleship is in the home.

Jesus' disciples were with Him the whole time. They lived with Him; ate with Him; went to weddings with Him; ministered to the people with Him; asked Him all manner of questions when they didn't understand the parables He was telling them. In fact, when Judas—the twelfth Apostle of the Lamb (Revelation 21:14)—needed to be replaced (Acts 1), one of the qualifications for the replacement was that he was to have been with Jesus and the other disciples *"all the time in which the Lord Jesus came in and went out amongst us"* (LITV). He had to have been one of the many other disciples who followed Him, but who were not mentioned as one of the twelve.

So, if we look more purposefully into the life of Jesus, we can see that Jesus conducted His discipleship **in the home**. And everywhere else, of course. He trained them in the ways of the new Kingdom. He gave them some instruction, mostly in the form of a parable, explained and instructed them in the meaning of the parable, corrected their lack of understanding, equipped them with His Spirit, and sent them out to do the same work He was doing on the earth. He modeled the way of the new kingdom; the new way of living that did not depend on following the written laws but on the laws of the heart that were dependent on the Spirit within.

Education vs Training

So, what is *training*? How is it different from *education*?

"Training is the process of changing behaviour."

Training shouldn't be confused with *correction* or *discipline*, both of which will be discussed later. Training is a process whereby we recognise *current behaviour* (Point A), quantify **desired behaviour** (Point B), and make an organised, informed, and rational plan to get from Point A to Point B. Training is designed to produce outcomes that can be **seen** and **measured**, such as cleaning our teeth. Training involves predictable outcomes in both skills and behaviours. Sometimes, there are levels of required skills or knowledge. So often we, as parents, react to the immediate situation at hand. When things are out of control, we then go into corrective mode or punish the pants off the dear little creatures, because we've reached our boiling point.

Training is a more continual, repetitive, and often physically demanding, process. Over an eighteen to twenty-year period, our goal is to move our children from having an external control mechanism to an internal one. When they're little, we first help them clean their teeth, then we tell them to go and clean their teeth, and then it becomes part of a daily morning and bedtime routine. As an adult, they are fully appreciative of having clean teeth and are internally motivated.

The Training Process

The goal of all training is to change behavior; this includes attitude, skills and knowledge. This is more than a one-time event; it is a process that takes place over time. The process of training (moving the learner from the Current Behavior to the Desired Behavior) needs a plan. The plan will include identifying the Current Behavior (although this is usually quite obvious!), describing the Desired Behavior (the actual attitude, skill or knowledge to be learned), deciding on the correction for inappropriate behaviour and the positive feedback to be given at the completion of the event.

Training Plan

Our Training Plan should be organised, informed, and rational. It should be logically thought through—not just a reaction as the day's activities unfold.

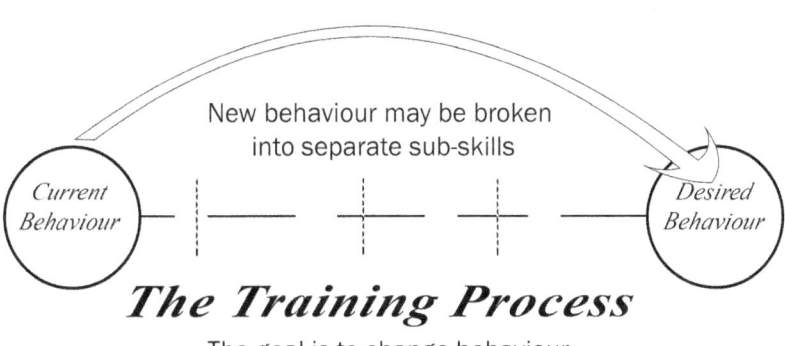

The Training Process
The goal is to change behaviour

The Training Plan, as you can see, has a definite beginning and a definite end. Current Behaviour is the beginning: it is the observable, current skills, knowledge or behaviour of the child. It may be an inappropriate behavior that needs correction (such as being cheeky), or it may be an immature attitude, skill or knowledge (such as how to set a table) that needs to be developed. The Training Plan identifies the gap between what is and what is required (indicated by the arrow).

The end of the process is the Desired Behaviour. It may be that which has already been determined for us in the Bible by Jesus (such as speaking respectfully) or it may be a cultural skill (such as setting a table).

The training process is our plan to move from Current Behaviour to Desired Behaviour. Sometimes, that training plan will need to be broken down into smaller chunks; sub-sets of the skill itself. For instance, if we want to teach our ten-month-old child to begin to clean his teeth, we first teach him to hold the toothbrush. We also show him how we do it. Much of our training is second nature to us, but if we think about the total task, we can see several smaller chunks such as holding the toothbrush, holding it up right, moving the brush up and down in the same direction as our teeth, turning the brush so that it can clean the back of our teeth, squeezing an appropriate amount of toothpaste, rinsing our mouth, and so on. Each of these subsets will take time to develop.

Correction, Discipline, Punishment and Reward

How does correction, discipline, and punishment fit in with training? What is the difference between each of them?

Correction is the process of putting someone back on track. This may be an attitude that needs correction; it may be behaviour; or, it may be something (a skill) that is being done. Where a child has a heart for doing the right thing, correction is easy. Often, it may just take a word. At other times, there may have to be a consequence so that the pain caused by the consequence causes a change in behaviour.

Discipline is the process of training in skills and behaviours. It is repetitive, often instructive, and produces an outcome. It involves regular and repetitive practice. Think of doing scales on a piano, speed drills in typing, or swimming laps. "Discipline" and "disciple" both come from the same root word. Discipline is not punishment!

As I've already shared, when I was a mum to my own family, I didn't understand the difference between these three vital aspects of training. In fact, I didn't understand much about having a family at all! I needed help and, unfortunately for all of us, the only help that was available was not very uplifting—to say the least. I was taught to "discipline" my children every time they were disobedient, even though my instructions were not always that clear. I was taught to confuse "discipline" and "punishment".

Punishment involves pain and is one of the greatest motivators for change. Many people don't agree with punishment, seeing it as a negative thing. It can very well be negative. When I now think of the word "punishment", I have a Dickensian mind picture of the mid-19th century, smoky, sleazy

London inner streets. The Roman schools of the 1st century used caning as punishment for not learning. It evokes the same mind picture in me and forces me to cringe on the inside, even though my mind now tells me there is a positive side to punishment. I have learned the positive aspects of punishment through a book, *Boundaries*, by Henry Cloud, John Pearson, John Townsend, Zondervan, 2008. I prefer not to use the word "punishment", using instead "consequences". Words have the power to affect our behaviour. When I use the word "consequence" with a child, it reminds me that I am in the "Training Event". It also helps them learn that their actions have consequences for which they are responsible.

Consequences are the result or effect of a certain behaviour; consequences can be both positive and negative. If I do a good deed for someone, I enjoy positive consequences. If I misbehave or do something bad, the consequences will be bad. When children learn that their actions have consequences, and that they are responsible for those actions, they begin to develop an internal "scaffolding" upon which all of their decisions will be based. This scaffolding will help them to internalise their motivation for change, increasing their level of maturity (over time).

These concepts will be used in describing the Training Event in more detail.

The Training Event Explained

In the training process, there is a handy saying that helps trainers remember a five-step process:

1. *I do, you watch*   We demonstrate the job
2. *I do, you help*   They do parts of the job under our directions
3. *You do, I help*   They do the whole job with us giving feedback
4. *You do, I watch*   They are now working independently
5. See you later, I'm outa here!

Step 1: I do, you watch. In the family, this is where our children see us for who we really are. Do we want to train them to read the Bible every day but neglect to do this ourselves? The greatest example we can give our children is the example they see us doing without us having to formally impart it to them. There's a word for this: "enculturation". This is the gradual acquisition of the characteristics and norms of the family (or another group). Another way to say this is *"The apple doesn't fall far from the tree"*.

When we are being purposeful with our training, we should begin each task with this step. We should allow the child to see how the task is performed by a competent person under normal circumstances. This gives them the "Point B" of the training task. They know where they are headed in the training and can often see the reward for the behaviour. It gives them a context and motivation for the task. What child growing up in a family doesn't aspire "be just like dad" (or mum)?

Step 2. I do, you help. This is where we give the child a small part in the overall process. I love to cook with my grandchildren. I give my 2-year-old the task of adding measured amounts into the mixture, but I give my 4-year-old the task of measuring those amounts. If I give either of them the task of mixing, I hold the spoon or the mixer, because their muscles are not developed enough to have sufficient control over the device.

During this process, feedback is important. It should be delivered constructively and with loving language and attitude. In the second part of the saying above, feedback is given so the child knows how they are going. This is where correction is given. Correction is *"a putting back on track"* when the learner has deviated from that track. It is part of the feedback. It should be a positive experience for the learner, not a negative one. Feedback also includes giving praise for a job well done. It is encouragement for the learner to proceed and helps build a sense of accomplishment. Feedback is part of relationship—and relationship is building. When I give encouragement and praise, boy, do they feel good about themselves!

Step 3. You do, I help. In the cooking example of the previous step, I allow the child to do a part of the process all by themselves. But when my friend's 12-year-old daughter comes to stay, I give her the recipe and the ingredients and let her do it all by herself, with me watching from somewhere within the kitchen. The encouragement and praise I give her is not as "over the top" (OTT) as I give the littlies, but I make sure that everyone who shares in the delights of her cooking knows who the cook is. Then I watch the proud, but shy, little smile that creeps over her face. I help by putting on the oven, getting out the trays, and watching over the process from a small distance.

In this step, the child is almost competent, but not quite able to be left on their own. During the process of training, we are the **external control mechanism** that is acting on the child. We are the ones guiding them in what they should learn and in what they should do. Eventually, though, we are wanting the control mechanism to change to an **internal control mechanism**. We want them to want to display the desired skill or behaviour.

Our job, as parents, is to adequately prepare our children for adulthood. Can you imagine an adult who doesn't clean their teeth, or make their bed, or wear clean clothes? We need to train our children to do all these things; we are the external control mechanism. Eventually, the motivation for doing these things comes from within. When that happens, our job is done. The child has reached maturity!

Step 4. You do, I watch. There isn't much difference between this stage and the previous one. It is more a matter of distance. While they do, we stand further and further away, occasionally come to check, and eventually, not at all. We may include a different context at this stage to see if they can transfer the skill they have just learned. For instance, they may do an excellent job at cleaning their teeth at home, but do they remember to clean their teeth on a sleep-over? They may be able to use a hand mixer to combine the eggs, but do they have the patience and the perseverance to mix egg whites until they are stiff and fluffy? This leads us on to the last stage.

We need to make sure, at this stage, that the demonstrated skill is consistent each time. We may also include understanding of social, health, and safety requirements. For instance, when making a cup of tea or coffee for an adult, why is it important to take the cup to the kettle and not the other way around? We also look for their ability to adapt. If they have been taught to make a cup of white tea, can they change the order to black tea? If a "pearl tea" is requested, and they've never heard of it before, can they ask for more information and then make it? If you've never heard of it before, a pearl tea is just hot water with a dash of milk.

Step 5. You're on your own! We are now confident that they can do the job. They have learned their skill so well, that they are able to transfer the skills into many different contexts. The skill can then be integrated into normal routine. With our foster kiddies, we used to say "Girls, its TTCB time". That meant it was time for them to pack up their current activity (they had 2-5 minutes in which to do that), then do **T**oilet, **T**eeth, **C**uddles and **B**ed. We had trained them in each of those activities (even in giving and receiving cuddles) and so the TTCB was just a phrase that set in motion a compete routine. This is an example of breaking down the Training Event into smaller, sub-set pieces before integrating those pieces into a whole event.

Reward

One of the biggest motivators for success is success itself. We know this. If we feel good about a certain achievement, we are encouraged to keep on achieving. It may be that we want to become better and achieve a higher result; it may be that we want to learn something new—because we feel sooooo clever!

Children are the same. When they are learning a new skill or behaviour, we need to shower them with praise and encouragement. If they are young, our praise can be really OTT. Initially, the reward itself will be the goal. When potty training, we might give a chocolate cooking drop for a wee and a larger chocolate (like a Freddo Frog here in Australia) for a poo. To start, the kiddies don't really care about doing their business in the potty. There's always been someone there to change their nappy for them, so why should they change? Oh, I get a chocolate? OK. I like chocolate. I'll give it a go.

Eventually, the external motivation (chocolate) changes into internal motivation as they begin to appreciate a clean and dry bottom and see how it pleases you, the one they love, when they do this. So, in our purposeful training regime, we need to understand that reward should be:

Directly linked to the behaviour ("Wow. Look at that. You just did a wee wee")

Given immediately (when it's all finished—"Great job; 'high five'. Come and get your chocolate")

Eventually, phased out to help your kiddie transition from the external reward to an internal reward (chocolate and a "high five" changes to just a "high five")

The same training and reward process can be used with all skills and behaviours. If trying to teach your kiddie to be gentle and loving to a new sibling, notice and reward good behaviour each time. "Oh look. You just gave your little sister/brother a kiss. That was very gentle and thoughtful of you. Well done. Let me give you a kiss."

So now we have looked at a Biblical model of discipleship. We have looked at how to train our children and to get the best from them. We've looked at the characteristics of a disciple so that we can know what behaviours we should be training into our children. Now it's time to look at ages and stages of growth so that we know what to do at any particular stage.

Stepping Stones to Maturity

Proverbs 22:6 *"Train up a child in the way he should go: and when he is old, he will not depart from it."*

In this chapter we will cover…

- The WHAT of child training

- The stages of development

- Specific strategies for incorporating discipleship into family life

This section is where the "rubber meets the road". This is where we tackle the "WHAT do I teach my kiddie?". I have such a heart of love for this little bundle of joy, but I wouldn't have a clue what to expect. If you're like I was, you're faced with nappies, maybe bottles, lack of sleep, a husband who wants his dinner (bless him), sore boobs, and "let downs" at the drop of a hat, and so much more. My mum, who only had one child, was on the other side of the country and not available for any kind of granny help. I had to find all this out on my own, so I feel your pain!

In this section, I'd like to show you what to do at each stage of your little bundle of joy's life. It's not an exhaustive list but more like a springboard for us to get going in the right direction. To give some structure to what I share, I'm using the *Early Years Learning Framework Practice Based Resource* document, funded by the Australian Government through their Department of Education, Employment and Workplace Relations. The document was developed to guide early childhood workers in their workplace as they work with children in childcare centres. You'll find the document in the reference section of this book.

Birth-4 months

Physically, our kiddies are developing all their muscles at this stage. They are such a joy to watch. They are also becoming little social butterflies. Some of them will make eye contact with everything that moves, and others will seem to flit away when a new contact is introduced. When the grandparents (grandies) come over, you'll often hear them say "Did you see that? She just smiled at me. I'll swear it wasn't wind!"

They learn to move their heads at the sound of a familiar voice and, when held, will peer intently at the face of whoever is holding them. Their biggest need, at this stage, is safety. They will develop their sense of safety and confidence through our responses to their cry for food and nappy changes. They instinctively develop the sense that they are loved and safe.

They begin to develop communication at an early age. Don't be surprised if you think you understand what your baby is trying to tell you—and don't second guess yourself. God has given mothers an awesome ability to understand non-verbal communication. In my experience, mothers look for signs such as increased crying, an arched back, a lack of response to sound, and many others, that some fathers just don't notice.

In Australia, we are fortunate to have many places of help for when we think we have a problem. Always seek the advice of professionals who can guide you through the developmental milestones.

We often under-estimate our baby's abilities at this stage. We think that, because they can't communicate, they don't understand. They certainly do. On a negative note, when there is conflict in the home, their sense of safety is greatly impaired. The difficulty for us is that the evidence for this doesn't show up until much later in life and we wonder why our children don't feel safe. We may not even be aware of the true root cause of their problems. We may just think that they are "shy" or "afraid of the dark" and that these things are "normal". They need not be normal.

Babies also respond well to music at this age. If we play worshipful or praise music, their whole brains respond. Did you know that music is the only activity in which the whole brain is actively engaged?

4-8 months

This is an interesting age where our baby's physical development can be seen almost on a daily basis. I always made sure they had floor time in ten-minute intervals, on a rug, where they learned to stretch out for objects of interest to them. I used to have brightly coloured, crumpled tissue paper that made a sound when touched. The colours attracted the baby and then the sound fascinated them. They may also have favourite toys that they reach out for more often, or that they may smile at when they see it.

Socially, they will respond more to familiar people and may show wariness to strangers. If Mom leaves the room, they may cry or fret. They haven't learned the concept of distance or time, yet, so if we're not there we're gone!

Play peek-a-boo with them to help develop their sense of distance and time.

When we're in another room, but still close by, we can sing songs or speak to them and tell them what we're doing. By hearing our voice, they will know that we are still there, even if they can't see us, and they will gain more confidence in their sense of safety

Introduce a variety of foods, especially savoury or non-sweet foods. Children who are fed vegetables at this age don't seem to question, at a later age, why vegetables form a large part of their diet

Spend one-on-one time communicating. During cuddle time, make sounds that your baby can copy to help them develop their speech. As you make a /b/ sound, watch them watching your mouth and trying to copy you.

Before each mealtime (when solids are introduced), say a quick prayer of thanks to Jesus for the food. Associate the prayer with an action, such as clapping, putting your hands together in the prayer mode, or lifting your arms in praise, so they associate the action with the prayer. Remember: we are making disciples of Jesus, not just raising kids.

8-12 months

Again, the physical development continues to astound grandies as they think there is no greater or more intelligent child on the planet than theirs! At this stage, we will have more brain space to begin to think about their training. There are still plenty of nappies, hubby still wants his dinner, and it's probably time we washed the floor (or swept it, at least!).

This is where it is appropriate to begin boundaries training—and before you ask, no, it isn't too early. The first boundary that needs to be learned is through the word NO. Children need to know what is socially acceptable and what isn't. They also need to know that we are boss, not them (and by "we", I mean both Mum and Dad).

At this age, noise becomes a big thing as they learn to bang different objects together. Some amount of noise is OK, because, among other things, it helps to develop a sense of rhythm which is so useful in formal learning at a later stage. But noise that drowns out any adult conversation should be a definite no-no and another chance for learning a boundary. They will also understand and respond to an increasing number of words.

Here are some ways to encourage useful development. They are not the only ways:

Sing songs that have finger actions, such as "Five little ducks went out one day…"

Sing the classic Jesus songs, such as "Jesus loves me this I know…" and use your own version of the actions

Clap your hands and they will copy. When you want them to have a good attitude toward something, such as prayer before a meal, clap your hands and show excitement ("Yay. It's prayer and dinner time"). When they respond favourably to something you want them to do, show your appreciation by clapping.

Wave your hands and they will copy. When Dad goes to work in the morning, wave goodbye to Dad and watch him leave. When he comes home, watch him arrive and show excitement with the clapping of your hands. This will show appreciation of Dad, and will also help your children to understand, at a later age, that Dad has been placed as the head of the home (according to Ephesians 5:23). A disciple needs to know the placement of Jesus as the head of the church and the placement of parents (through the headship of the husband) over children.

Language development continues as they say more and more words. I called my little grandchild a goose one day when she did something funny. For the next ten minutes or so she went around the house saying "goose…. goose…".

Instruct in safety. Choose one thing (to begin with) that you don't want your little joy doing or saying. It may be a safety issue, such as touching a power point, heater, or pedestal fan. Be deliberate in your instruction. Take your child to the object and, gently taking their hand close to the object, say NO. Withdraw their hand and then repeat the process several times. Each time you say NO, drop the tone of your voice so they can hear the difference (remember, they are learning about the sounds, volume, and tone of voice). We needn't be cross with the expression of NO, but serious, certainly, as they learn to hear the difference in tone.

For children who are more determined than others, and keep being attracted to the forbidden object, they should be redirected at first. Find another object that will attract them. If this doesn't work, you may have to be more serious when saying NO. Drop the tone of your voice even more. You may need to be quite stern, with some little bundles of joy. This change in tone will frighten some children and cause them to cry. You will know how far to go with your own child as you will be learning their particular personality and character traits. Most emphatically, we don't need to yell or raise our voice too loudly. We want to teach our children to respond to changes in tone and seriousness. We need to model with them the soft, quiet voice of instruction or direction that our Heavenly Father gives to us—and He never yells. When they begin to respond to your NO, reward them by showing excitement and, for some, giving a treat. The hardest thing for all of us, at this stage, is **consistency!** We will not only be teaching them not to touch whatever object we have chosen, but we will be setting the groundwork for the rest of our training program. Our little kiddie needs to know—beyond a shadow of a doubt—that we are the one who has the authority. Discipleship is about discipline—the regular practice of desired behaviours.

Once we have won that battle, we can begin to introduce other boundaries. We may also be able to soften our stern responses to a milder "Uh, uh!"—a reminder of the boundary we have previously set.

1-2 years

At this age, there is huge advance in the physical. They walk, they run, they bounce large balls, they feed themselves—but for all their curious and energetic play, they will still depend on adult reassurance. Their sense of identity will grow. Don't think we have to teach them independence. This is a wrong thought in society today. In making disciples, we need to teach our children *inter*dependence; we teach them to have faith and to rely on those over them, especially Jesus, but with a sense of personal responsibility. That may seem like an unrealistic expectation for children of this age, but this is when their autonomy begins to emerge.

When feeding in a highchair, give them their own teaspoon so they can learn the art of feeding while you get on with the business of feeding.

Allow them to practice with a pencil or crayon but teach them that there is a special place for drawing (at a table) and that "we only draw on paper". This phrase becomes a learning signal that will help them to develop boundaries. At first, they will probably swap the crayon or pencil from hand to hand as they learn hand dominance.

Playing with other children is important at this stage. Initially, they will play alongside other children without deliberate interaction. This is called "parallel play". This is when they can learn to share toys as well as mum's presence. They should also develop care, empathy and respect for others.

Emotionally, they may need more reassurance. As they begin to focus on the outside world, they need to come back to a safe place. When they fall over, or when they are upset, the first thing to do is to cuddle and reassure the child.

Then you can find out what the problem is. I like to think that each child has an "emotional tank" which we fill up for them as we cuddle them and give them emotional assurance. As they go out to explore their world, their tank "leaks" and they need it filled up again.

Night time presents a challenge for a new parent. At this age, our little kiddies often lose control at the busiest time of the day. We are busy preparing dinner, bathing, preparing for Dad to come home; if we have older children, they may also be doing homework. A little forward planning can help ease our workload. Try to prepare and/or cook dinner earlier in the day. This can be a great help in reducing the workload for this busy time. Have a regular "cuddle time" or story time for five or ten minutes to reassure them and re-centre their focus back onto the home environment.

PARENT: "What's next?"

CHILD: "Wipe my bottom"

PARENT: "What's next?"

CHILD: "Pull up my pants"

PARENT: "What's next?"

CHILD: "Press the button"

PARENT: "What's next?"

CHILD: "Wash my hands"

PARENT: "What's next?"

CHILD: "Dry my hands"

PARENT: "What's next?"

CHILD: (In the early stages, a reward for doing the right thing)

PARENT: "What's next?" "Go and play"

PARENT: "What's next?" "Well done!"

We also need to teach our children to communicate their feelings. When they feel tired and grumpy, they will often cry or whinge. It is important to begin with a reassuring cuddle and follow it up with "Use your words, honey." This will help them to begin to regulate their emotions. We don't want to turn them into bricks of ice where emotions are concerned but we do want them to learn self-control (within age-appropriate guidelines).

Much learning takes place through playing games. For household activities, such as toilet training, turn it into a game. Here is a game I played with my nephew when he was learning toilet training. We called it the "What's next?" game and it didn't take him long to develop good toilet manners.

Learning to pick up toys can also be done through playing games. Placing toys in a basket or other container can be done by saying "one for you" as the child places a toy in the basket and "one for me" as the parents places a toy in the basket. This teaches the child cooperation, reinforces the concept of "self" as distinct from "others", and personal responsibility.

2-5 years

Training is a lot more intentional now. Our little bundles of joy are now demonstrating a distinct and delightful personality. This is where our discipleship training begins in earnest. There will be many physical developments during these years. They will mature socially, emotionally, and cognitively (their capacity to think and reason).

At this age, children don't question whether or not Jesus exists. If Mom or Dad talk about Jesus, then He must exist. It's not until children go to school that they begin to think Mom and Dad don't know everything. But if we have laid the foundation of discipleship, even school will not destroy that. Be aware, though, that they may have a conflict of thought that will need addressing. They may recognise that Mom and Dad believe one thing and school believes another—especially in the areas of creation versus evolution, and sexuality or "gender fluidity". This usually happens in the next stage of development, after six years of age; but be prepared at any earlier stage, if necessary.

At bedtime, pray to Jesus. We begin by praying for our child to demonstrate how to pray. As this becomes part of the bedtime routine, it will also become part of the emotional stability that gives reassurance to our child. After some months, we may like to pray together. We say a phrase and have our child repeat what we say. Later, they can add suggestions for what to pray. In this way, we teach our child how to pray. We may also teach our child The Lord's Prayer from Matthew 6.

We read the Bible stories to our children and talk about the characters in the stories. Talk about right and wrong from this story. Children are beginning to develop their sense of right and wrong and we need to teach them that the standard for right and wrong is based on the Word of God, not on what we think. Ask them questions about the Bible story. This develops their cognitive ability, gives us feedback about what they are thinking, and develops their ability to think analytically—although they won't be sufficiently competent in thinking analytically until high school years.

Children of this age are also beginning to show guilt or remorse for disobedience. This is when we can teach our children about true repentance. Chapter 5 talks about how to correct inappropriate behaviour.

In Chapter 2 Discipleship, one of the characteristics of a disciple is that they are quick to be obedient. Obedience should not be taught as a form of control. Obedience is the way in which we demonstrate our submission to another person. As a disciple, we need to submit to God and His ways. This is the primary purpose of obedience. Personal safety is another reason. If we say, "don't touch", we may need instant obedience for our children's personal safety. When they are obedient, this not only keeps them safe, but increases their emotional security. If children are not obedient to parents whom they can see, how on earth can they learn obedience to a God whom they can't see.

Begin teaching Bible memory verses such as John 3:16. Not only does this give the child a good grounding in the Word of God, it also helps develop memory skills that will be useful later on in school. Make it a fun activity. Turn it into a song. Take turns in saying some words in the memory verse, a little bit like filling in the blank. Don't be surprised if your child learns quicker than you! My foster children learned the whole passage in 1 Corinthians 11:23-26 in a matter of days as we celebrated this before our meal each night—just through repetition. When we realised this, we involved them a lot more in the leading of the celebration.

Read the Bible together every day. Just a short passage to begin with, increasing as the child gets older. There are many Bibles available for children, from small picture books to modern language versions that are age appropriate. By reading and praying together each day, you will be teaching your child consistency. You will also be giving your child the opportunity to bear fruit as a disciple. It's wonderful for them to see that, as issues arise and are brought to Jesus in prayer, He also gives us answers. They get the opportunity to see healings taking place through regular prayer and their faith grows as a result. We can also teach them to give thanks as they see the answers to prayer.

The Chapter 2 Discipleship also talked about reporting back. We need to teach children to report back when they have been given a job or a message. In these preschool years, we can give our children simple jobs to do, such as wiping the dishes, packing or unpacking the dishwasher, putting their dirty clothes in the basket, etc. This helps teach them personal responsibility and contributes to the teamwork of the family. Following the principals in the Training Event from the chapter on Discipleship, when our child has been taught a certain task, we can then leave them on their own to finish the task but to report back to us when that task is finished and to ask if it is done to your satisfaction. Don't forget to reward for a job well done!

Help children to develop a decision-making framework. Begin by giving them small choices. "What would you like on your sandwich?" and, particularly for girls, "Which of these two dresses would you like to wear?". When beginning to give a two-year-old a choice, don't be tempted to ask a more general question, such as "What would you like to wear today?" as we haven't yet developed framework for them in which a decision can be made. This more general question gives the child more autonomy than they can handle at this age. The importance is not what the child wears but on developing a framework. In the process toward maturity, we first need to learn obedience.

Someone else (a parent or teacher) sets the standard or framework. The next stage is to learn to make a choice within a predefined framework, or set of standards, such as having a shower before or after dinner (age appropriate, of course). The final stage is when our children are old enough, and mature enough, to set the framework or the standard, such as which bill to pay first. When we are adults, hopefully, we are well prepared to set a framework for our own children to follow. This is the practical outworking of 2 Timothy 2:2: *"And the things you have heard from me among many witnesses, commit these to faithful men who will be able to teach others also"*. The teacher (in this case the parent), sets the framework, commits (teaches) it to the faithful men (the children), and the faithful men (children) become the parent who are able to teach it to others.

As I was growing up, I heard it said, "Give me a child before he's eight and I'll give you a good Catholic!". Here in Australia, at least at the time of writing, we have the freedom to volunteer as a Christian Religious Instructor in State Primary Schools for up to 1 hour each week. In practice, we are given one half hour lesson. I have observed that as the children from non-Christian homes go up in grade levels they also go down in their belief and acceptance of God. They learn to take on the world's standards and become anti-God because the process of discipleship is not happening—even in some Christian families.

If we want to bring up our children in the "nurture and admonition of God" (Ephesians 6:4) it must begin at an early age. But this is more than just teaching. Discipleship is a lifestyle. It must be demonstrated in the home. Mom and Dad must also commit to being disciples of Jesus. They must demonstrate the characteristics of accountability, submission, and reporting back before they can be sent "on mission" to their own children. And then, what a joy it is to travel the discipleship journey together as a family!

We have looked at a few strategies for developing a lifestyle of discipleship within the home. I'm sure you'll come up with many more as you live life, read books, and talk to other Moms. This chapter is only a springboard from which to jump into motherhood. We now need to look at boundaries, choice and consequences and how these simple concepts can bring our children into greater maturity.

Boundaries, Choice and Consequence

Colossians 4:6b *"Choose your words carefully and be ready to give answers to anyone who asks questions."*

In this chapter we will cover...

- How consequences are linked to the choices we make
- The importance of making choices
- A simple Boundaries concept
- The NO Boundary
- Family roles and responsibilities
- Some suggested simple boundaries
- Different parenting styles
- Clear communications

Choice and Consequence

When my children were growing up, as I said in the introduction, I didn't have a clue! One of the things I learned along the way was that every choice has a consequence. When my teenagers were growing up, we had a saying in our family — "You can choose your actions, but you can't choose your consequences!". I taught my children (notice I didn't say "trained"!) that every choice has an inbuilt consequence. If you jump out of a tree or a plane, there is only one way (consequence) and that is — Down! Gravity works! There is a physical law in place that we can't see. In the same way, whenever we make a choice, there is a spiritual law in action even though we can't see it. We can't see the physical law of gravity, only its result; we can't see the spiritual laws, but they are there. If we make a good choice, we will get a good result; if we make a bad choice, we will get a bad result.

When I learnt about choice and consequence, I thought I was ahead of the game. I knew I was really onto something. My kids hated hearing, "You can choose your actions, but you can't choose your consequences." because we would repeat that phrase every time that they did something wrong. As you can see, I hadn't really learnt the difference between teaching and training. And I didn't have a clue about boundaries until most of them had grown up and left home.

I eventually read a very helpful book on *Boundaries*, written by Dr Henry Cloud and Dr John Townsend. As I read through this book, I began to put into practice the concept of boundaries. It was wonderful. I felt empowered. I was more confident about who was in control of my life. No longer did I need to react to the whims of other people.

I learned to implement boundaries with a young friend. She used to live in town, a little off the main road and on my way to work. I would normally leave home at 8am for an 8:30am start. Sometimes, she would phone just on 8am to say she had slept in, and to ask for a lift to work. It was convenient for both of us, because she worked just opposite to my place of work. It was only a 10-minute deviation out of my way to go to her house, and I enjoyed seeing her.

While we were in the car together, we talked about a lot of things. It was good having adult conversation with this young woman. I began to tell her what I had been learning about in the *Boundaries* book, but she was completely resistant to what I had to tell her. I felt that I wasn't doing a good job because she kept on bringing up what she thought was a scenario where boundaries wouldn't work. (You know how we women become all emotional and think the problem is with us!) It began to dawn on me that, on the days that I picked up my young friend, I often had to speed in order to get to work on time. I realised, with the help of Doctors Cloud and Townsend, that her being late did not justify my speeding. I also realised that it would be me who would pay the speeding fine and not her—even though I wasn't the reason why we were late.

I decided to broach the subject with her (with some trepidation, I might add, as she had a very forthright way of expressing herself). We spoke about it in the car and I told her, firmly but politely, I needed her to phone before 7:45am. She was very agreeable (and that should have been my first clue!). However, the next time she phoned it was 8am, and I reminded her of our conversation and how we had agreed she should phone before 7:45am.

She tried sweet talking me, but I was firm. I was establishing a boundary. Well! Did she get cross! She slammed down the phone in the middle of our conversation and I didn't hear from her for about a week.

She came to visit the next Sunday afternoon while my husband and I were entertaining our neighbours. They were confiding in us what was happening in their son's marriage. They were so hurt by the circumstances that not even my friend's presence deterred them. And then — "out of the mouths of babes"! — my friend piped up and said that they should be setting boundaries in the relationship. I listened to her describe a boundary and how they could all use them in the relationship problems they were describing. Not only had she been listening, but she did an awesome job of describing boundaries to our neighbours and they were listening intently to all she had to say.

I learned something that day. I learnt that when I set a boundary, I'm not responsible for the other person's reaction; I also learned that, although I thought my friend was resistant, she wasn't really. She had been listening all the time, and just vocalised possible objections to new information to help herself sort out and process the new information.

When choice and consequence are working properly, we are helping to build personal responsibility in our children. Children who grow up learning personal responsibility will be more mature, well-adjusted, and resilient.

Remember the Training Event that was mentioned in the Chapter 2 Discipleship? As a parent, we observe their current behaviour. This behaviour is age-related and, usually, culturally dependent. We also have the maturity to decide what the desired behaviour should be. It is the role of both mother and father to determine the desired behaviour and the training process. The roles and responsibilities of each member of the family need to be clearly understood and clearly set by both parents.

We've all heard of the "terrible twos". This period in a child's life may begin as early as 12 to 18 months old. It may not end until they are closer to 3 years old. Most parents want to tear their hair out at this stage! But with a little understanding and planning we can actually be victorious. I don't use that word lightly (victorious) because it often feels like a battle that we are losing — to a two-year-old Ninja Toddler!

Children of this age can be willful, stubborn, and tantrum prone. Gone is that cute little angel and in its place is a monster we don't recognise. We ask them what they want for breakfast, they ask for toast; then we find it on the floor, or worse, on the wall. Children of this age are learning to make decisions. They **did** decide to eat toast. That was their first decision. And then they made another decision — to **not** eat toast — but their communication and cognitive skills are not sufficiently advanced, so they have difficulty expressing themselves. They know something is wrong, but they don't know how to fix it. That's where the tantrum comes in.

Another common place for tantrums is at the supermarket. This is where we definitely feel a victim to blackmail! Sitting in the trolley, our little angel has a good view of all that is on the shelf. Supermarkets deliberately plan their product placement to take advantage of this. They point to a brightly coloured package, or they ask for their favourite sugar-coated cereal, and smile sweetly to us but, when we say NO or are distracted and don't answer, the tantrum hits 8.0 on the Richter scale and we receive knowing looks from other parents in the supermarket.

So how do we handle this?

Making Choices

All good training begins in the home. We train them to make choices. We learn the difference between an "open" and a "closed" question. An open question is designed to gather as much information as possible. The answer to an open question comes from a wide range of experiences which our little angels definitely don't have.

A closed question is used to clarify information. For example, "What would you like for breakfast?" is an open question. It gives our little angel the freedom to request Eggs Benedict, Forest Fruit Compote, or a range of other dishes that are definitely not on the menu. Thankfully, these delectable dishes are usually also not part of the experience from which they can draw an answer.

But if we say, "Would you like toast or cereal?" we have given a choice between two alternatives. Our toddler is much more likely to cope with a choice between two alternatives. They are also much more likely to be happy with the consequence. This provides a framework within which they can learn to make decisions. It also provides a positive framework within which boundaries may be established. As they progress in the decision-making framework, they may say they want a third alternative. We now have a range of responses to consider. First, we can then teach them to ask politely for the third alternative and decide whether or not it is a feasible option. This teaches them the skill of negotiation. Secondly, we may recognise signs of anger in their demand for a third alternative. Some strong-willed children may care more about getting their own way than they care about what they eat. Thirdly, a whining tone may indicate a desire to control through manipulation.

When that second decision kicks in (the one that says "I don't want to eat toast") we can firmly, but kindly, remind them they asked for it. When they insist that they don't want toast (which they surely will do at some stage) we can say "Ok.", wipe their hands and get them down from the chair.

They will soon learn that, when a decision has been made, they need to be responsible for the decision. Of course, we always have one who absolutely refuses to play the game and will use every trick in their little book to get their own way.

At first, I began to hate the confrontation that this "battle of the wills" produced. Then, someone older and wiser than me pointed out that I was blessed to have a "strong-willed child" because he/she would not be led astray by peer pressure as a teen. It was amazing how a changed attitude also changed the outcome.

What are Boundaries?

Think of a fence around our property. The fence delineates what we are responsible for. We mow the grass inside the fence, because this is our responsibility; we don't mow our neighbour's lawn, because that is their responsibility.

Boundaries work in the same way in the intangible parts of our life. As parents, we establish behaviours we will except and what we won't accept. We also teach our children about boundaries. We initiate acceptable behaviour and then teach our children to internalise those behaviours.

For instance, young children need to know what belongs to them and what belongs to others. It is a good "Christian" principle to teach little children to share. Right? It is, but we can only share what we know belongs to us.

If children don't have a strong sense of ownership over their toys, they can't make that choice to share. There are two aspect to this: First is the sense of ownership. When that is strong it leads to a sense of security. Second is the ability to make a choice.

Although we want our children to share, we need to respect their choice if they decide not to share. It isn't because they are being mean or not wanting to share. It is because they are still developing their sense of ownership and boundary control.

It may sound like a silly statement, but we can't teach boundaries if they don't operate in our own lives.

As a young adult, I learned to cross a very busy four-lane highway in peak traffic. I was so clever; I didn't need to use a pedestrian crossing! But all that changed when I had children. I found myself using a pedestrian crossing as an example to my children and became angry with other adults who didn't follow my practice when they were with my children.

Nobody told me to do this. It was my parent's previous training that just kicked in. It became my internal motivation. We can't give what we don't have!

So, the first step, in implementing boundaries, is to make sure they are established within ourselves first.

The NO Boundary

One of the first boundaries that a child should learn is the word NO. NO is also the first boundary word we can teach them. This is not a politically correct word, these days, but it is still vital that children learn this word and what it means. How many times do toddlers reach out for things that can harm them? A fan, a heater, a pot on the stove? If they don't respond to this word — a warning, really! — they can suffer serious consequences.

This simple word is one of the first words a child may learn to speak. Some parents hate hearing their little darling use that word back to them — and rightly so — because it usually means another battle of the wills is about to begin, so let's put this into context.

When we say NO to our children, we are usually saying it out of a place of authority. I am assuming that we have a good attitude with our children and are not just saying it to be capricious. That sort of parenting never works! I'm also assuming that you, dear reader, are not that sort of parent. You wouldn't be reading this book if you were.

We may also be saying NO out of a place of safety. When our little toddler is just about to do something dangerous, we often don't have time for a full sentence, but must get their attention and compliance quickly. If the groundwork has already been laid, our toddler will respond to a short, sharp NO, because it will be so different from how we normally talk to them. It will be, in these times, that they are developing their sense of trust versus mistrust.

Our toddler's world is a place of immensely unpredictable things all around. They need to know, "If I cry, will someone come help me?". Stability and consistency of care are vital to their maturity. It is from this place that we need to say NO at the appropriate time.

When our children say NO to us, it is very different. Children learn to control their world at an early age. Our toddler, as I said in the previous paragraph, needs a sense of security, stability and trust. If they don't feel it (something they can't articulate or quantify) they try to control the world around them for their own safety. This is what is happening at a psychological level; but on a physical level, it looks quite different! It looks like a toddler out of control; a toddler throwing an 8.0 tantrum (on the Richter scale for tantrums) or battle of the wills. We need to recognise when and how these battles begin.

Our communication needs to be consistent, gentle, reliable, predictable and clear so that our boundaries are understood, well establish and create a sense of trust and solidity for our toddler. God has entrusted our children to our care and has graced us with the knowledge, skills and love that they need. Parenting is a stewardship and the "boss", for whom we are employed as a steward, is our Father. When giving instructions, we may have asked "Do you want to …. (eat your breakfast?)". This gives our toddler the chance to say NO. When we say "I want you to …. (eat your breakfast)" this gives them the chance to be obedient and compliant. The first question allows them to respond with what they want (or don't want) to do; the second statement is a clear statement of what behaviour is expected of them.

A Developing NO

NO and DON'T are words that establish boundaries and respect. "Don't play with my phone." is something a child needs to be taught at an early age. But as they learn that we place restrictions on them, they also can learn that they can place restrictions on others (as appropriate). They can ask siblings not to play with their toys. This develops a sense of ownership and responsibility. Children need to learn this as well as how to share. Teaching a child not to play with Mum's or Dad's phone is teaching them about ownership and responsibility. I see many parents whose young and teenage children just take over their parent's phone as if they have a "right". Boundaries teach us that, with a right, comes the responsibility of ownership.

We played a lot of tickling games with our children. There was nothing they loved to do more than to roll around on the carpet with Dad, being tickled, and trying to tickle Dad. It was a family affair — all in together. The older children learned to tickle the younger ones; they learned to be gentle; they learned to respect NO if a younger one had had too many tickles. I'm glad to report that this was a family affair that was conducted in full sight of everyone — otherwise, we could be facing accusations from some well-meaning adult that wasn't even there!

How did we become so politically correct and super-sensitive to the possible evil consequences?

Family Roles and Responsibilities

Children also need to learn their place in the pecking order. As this is a book on discipleship, and we are discipling our children to Jesus, we need to teach them their place in the body of Christ. According to Colossians 1:18, Jesus is the head of the church. That's not too hard to accept. When we go to church on Sundays, we may hear about the headship of Jesus. Ephesians 1:22 also says that Jesus is *"head over everything"*. But in chapter 5, we also read that, in the family, the husband is *"head of the wife in the same way that*

Jesus is head of the church". Again, this is not politically correct but it's what the Word of God says.

The husband is the head of the family. This means that he has the guardianship of the family. He is to act as the spiritual shepherd, providing sustenance for his sheep, protecting them against evil, and caring for them in a loving relationship. In this, he is demonstrating the guardianship of Jesus over His church. When Jesus returned to heaven, he left us His spirit to be our helper, to enable us to carry out His requirements. In the same way, when Dad goes to work each day, he leaves his wife to be his helper in the house, to enable the children to carry out his requirements. In Genesis 2:18 and 20, God calls the wife a *"helper"* because it has always been His intention that the wife help the husband to establish a family unit that is submitted, committed and accountable to Jesus as disciples.

So, it is in this context that we need to teach children to respectfully interact with other adults and children. Establishing firm and secure boundaries provides our children with a framework within which they can grow and mature.

One practical way in which we can help our children develop boundaries is through play. Children learn through play, so it makes sense that, if we want to teach them something, the best environment is one of play. Toddlers love Mom or Dad to sit on the floor and build blocks. See who can build the biggest tower, then have fun rolling a ball into the tower to see who knocks it down (but make sure all the valuables and breakable objects are up high!). There is so much learning involved in this simple activity: manual dexterity and manipulation, colours and shapes, height, competition (within a healthy framework), ball skills, taking turns, laughing, relationship building, sharing and just generally having fun.

For preschool children, use a pack of cards to play Go Fish. This game develops gross and fine motor skills, increases their social skills, increases their ability to take turns, helps develop visual clues and emotions, develops transactional language, develops shape discrimination and number recognition, and, again, is just good fun.

Boundaries Examples

The following is a list of some basic behaviours to teach children that will increase their sense of boundaries and provide a foundation for more advanced behaviours. It is not an exhaustive list but one that can be used a springboard for more training.

Use manners: "Please" when requesting something and "Thank you" when it is received. Even very young children can be taught these basic manners. Don't receive anything from the child unless these two words are used. We can have high expectations of our children but be relational in the way we deliver those expectations.

Display "company manners": We used the phrase "company manners" to describe the behaviour that was expected when we were out or when we had visitors. We made sure our children were trained in table manners—how to use the cutlery and napkin, how to chew with a closed mouth, and how to not talk with food in the mouth. We also taught them that, when we go too another person's house, they are only allowed to eat the food offered to them; also, that they didn't have to ask us if they were allowed to take what was offered each time they were offered food. They knew they could have two biscuits or one piece of cake without asking us for permission. This gave them a sense of autonomy but within socially acceptable guidelines. We also kept an eye on their play, not allowing them to run riot in the excitement of being with a friend. This surveillance was also kept up in the shops, in church and other public places. If any of them were getting a little too loose with their behaviour, we only had to say "company manners" and they knew exactly what to do.

Sit to eat: Do we really want food or drink spilled everywhere else in the house? Sitting in a highchair, at the table, or even on the kitchen floor teaches that child that there is *"A place for everything, and everything in its place"*. It aids digestion; and gives a sense of belonging, i.e. food belongs in this place.

Pick up toys: This teaches is our child responsibility — my toys, my job. It also helps the child to develop a sense of organisation. I have achieved much better results, especially with children who are finding it hard to be organised and those with developmental delays, to organise different groups of toys into different storage containers. I have one very large plastic container for the Lego, a small container for little cars and trucks, another container for jigsaws which are each in a separate closable plastic bag, and so on. The jigsaws are done at a table within easy reach of where I am working and when we have finished with one jigsaw, it goes back into its plastic bag and another one comes out. When the jigsaws are finished, the box goes back and out comes the next activity. These may seem a little OTT but, trust me, when you have five children (not to mention their friends who are visiting) it's much easier on the parent when clean up time comes.

Wear one set of clothes per day: I have seen so many mothers allow their children to access their clothes at any time of day. If the sleeves of their T-shirts get wet when they wash their hands after going to the toilet, they simply go and change their whole outfit — or sometimes, just because they want to. The previous set of clothes may or may not end up in the wash basket! I don't know about you, but I don't have time to do this much washing. This is where the permissive parenting is counterproductive.

Help with house jobs: With preschool children, I don't expect them to do any regular job, but they have delighted in being with me as I do my jobs — sometimes to the point of frustration! As I vacuum the floor, my toddler wants to take over the vacuuming. I let them use the vacuum with me and, as I push forward, I say "forward" and then "backward" when we go backwards (teaching direction). Mostly, they only want to do this for a couple of minutes before they become distracted with something else. If they want to do it some more, I give them the vacuum and stand back and watch. Yes, it takes longer to do the job, but it also amuses, as well as trains, our children. For my school age children, I usually gave them one small job each day. This was more for the sake of teaching discipline and responsibility.

Speak respectfully: Our children need to understand how to speak respectfully to both adults and children. If they are respectful to others, they will find that others are respectful toward them. When there is a dispute over a toy, we often hear "Give it back!", but, if ownership of the requesting child has been properly established, we can coach our child to say, "That is my toy and I would like you to give it to me, please". Similarly, we can coach the sibling to respect the first child's ownership and to respectfully give it back. Often, the second child has taken the toy without asking and this is where the offence has started. It takes great wisdom and skill in asking questions to determine where the offence began. I was fortunate enough to be a trainer in the retail industry, training others in providing customer service. I was taught how to ask questions of the customer, especially in complaint matters, so that an adequate and fair resolution could be made. Complaints always ended up in the manager's office, so it was a skill I learned quickly in my career. I automatically transferred these skills into my parenting.

Treat animals with care: I had one child in my care who could not empathise with the needs and feelings of others. Having a pet helped her to learn gentleness, self-control and responsibility. I am so saddened when I hear stories of children being cruel to animals.

Try different foods: Not only does this make our kitchen duties much easier, but it also helps our children to be willing to take a risk. I am not advocating the kind of risk that makes our children unsafe. Have you ever noticed that "successful" people in life, at some point in their lives, had to take a risk? It was this risk-taking that allowed them to break through whatever barrier was holding them back from their personal success. This is one of those times when we don't want to have expectations that are too high. We only want to encourage the trying beforehand, and then rewarding afterward, regardless of the outcome.

Eat vegetables: I am staggered, sometimes, when I see young children only eating carbohydrate food. Their diet is full of chips, biscuits, spaghetti, macaroni cheese, cereal, or bread. There is so much information available on healthy diets that there is no excuse for this behaviour. You may be thinking that I am a bit hard, and maybe I am, but I have lived long enough to see the end results. I know a child who, over a few years, developed the habit of only eating foods that were white. I encouraged the mother to seek professional help for this child. At the time of writing, she is now a young adolescent and beginning to try other foods but is still extremely limited in food choice and beginning to suffer in health. Thankfully, this suffering is producing motivation to try other, healthier foods.

Follow a routine: It may feel strange to read and that I am advocating both risk-taking and routine. They may seem to be polar opposites. There are many studies that demonstrate the healthy effect of a routine for children. Think of life from a child's point of view: the world outside of their home can be a big, scary place. They need the love and protection that is provided by Mum and Dad. This makes them feel safe and secure. Within this framework, they feel safe enough to take small risks. Children will not take a risk unless they have a history of feeling safe and secure from a younger age. A predictable routine provides the safety and security they need.

Limit technology: I seem to be staggered a lot! I was staggered to hear from Brad Huddleston on YouTube (he wrote a book called "Digital Cocaine") that primary schools in Silicon Valley do not you use computers in the classroom. If I had thought about it before I heard Brad Huddleston speak, I would have thought that Silicon Valley would have been leading the way in using computers in the classroom. Here in Australia, our schools are being told how essential it is to have a computer in the classroom "for education". According to Brad Huddleston, there is no difference between being addicted to technology and being addicted to cocaine as far as our brain is concerned. No parent in their right mind would allow their children to use cocaine. And yet, we allow our children hours of unrestricted use on TV, iPad, computer, and smart phone — even up to 6-8 hours a day. I understand the argument that our children need to "keep up" with their peers but, particularly if there is already a computer at school, we need to limit all forms of technology in the home. My personal observation is that children who grow up with unlimited technology actually display signs of being less intelligent and creative because they are waiting for (a brightly coloured) someone to tell them what to think or what to do.

Display personal hygiene: This is a no-brainer! We don't want to be changing the nappy of our ten-year-old. We don't even want to be washing nappies after our little cherub has passed the two-year stage. Having five children — all of whom were about two years apart—I look back on my life and count ten years of breast feeding and nappy washing! I know, disposable nappies have made the job a lot easier, but they haven't entirely taken away the washing burden. Anyway, a child with good personal hygiene is one who has a good self-image.

Recognise consequences: Here, I mean more than just telling our kids "You can choose your actions, but you can't choose the consequences". I mean that we need to consciously train this into our children in a fun, and a relational way. For instance, as our child is on a step or ledge, and they want to jump off that ledge, we can ask them, "What do you think will happen? Will you go "up" or "down"? What do you think?" After they laugh at how silly you are for thinking they might go "up", you can hold their hand and encourage them to jump. Then we might say "Wow! You were right. We did go down. How did you get to be so smart?" Another scenario may be to show them on the internet (if you don't have access to a real farm) how a drought on a farmer's land (one they don't even know) may mean we can't have milk on our cereal for breakfast.

Moving on from this, when we have told our child not to do something and we can see they are tempted to do it, we can ask them, "What do you think will be the consequence if you go ahead and do it after I've already said NO?" When they give an answer, we then give them a choice — and follow up on the consequence! Particularly if it is a good choice, we can encourage them for making that good choice.

Read books, especially the Bible: We can begin reading children's Bibles and storybooks. As our children grow older, we can read to them from an easy-to-understand version of the Bible and watch them develop a keenness for reading the Bible themselves.

Become a storyteller: Insert "Oooh" and "Oh, no" at the right place and watch their reaction to the story. This can become part of the bedtime routine. We may even find that, without the distractions of the day, our children will begin to talk to us about problems they are encountering. This is a very precious part of our life together.

There is also a wonderful book called "Honey for a Child's Heart" written by Gladys Hunt. One of the things that Hunt says in her book is "*'This is what a book does. It introduces us to people and places we wouldn't ordinarily know. Books are experiences that make us grow, that add something to our inner stature*".

Hunt shows how reading affects our children's view of the world and their imagination. I remember reading this book about forty years ago. One of the things I remember is how a child's imagination affects their understanding of what is read to them.

We had just been introduced to "The Lion, The Witch and the Wardrobe" by CS Lewis. It was also showing on TV as a serial cartoon. We made it part of our Friday night family activity and were excited about watching it together as we had almost finished reading the book in our bedtime routine. Watching the TV show, my eight-year-old boy was fine, and my six-year-old boy was fine (although at times, he needed to sit closer to dad). My four-year-old girl, who knew and coped with the story from our family reading, was distracted during the TV show and had nightmares every Friday night. I realised, from reading Hunt's book and from watching the TV show, that a visual image for a young child is a much stronger influence on them than their own imagination, because their life experience is so limited, and they can only bring to the reading of a book an image they have already encountered.

Today, I see many parents allowing their children to watch movies that would psychologically affect adults and I am saddened to know the, almost-certain outcome for the child. A child is not able to separate reality from fiction until around eight years of age, so the visual images that come to them from a screen seem all too real to them. They don't know anything about computer-generated imagery (CGI) and just accept that what they see is real.

Listen to music: I learned a song in Sunday School (two actually) that have formed the basis of my Christian life. The first one was "Jesus Loves Me This I Know" and the second one was "The Best Book to Read is the Bible". Early childhood education is full of songs and rhymes. Children love the familiarity, the repetition and the predictability of a song—not to mention the beat and melody! One of the best song series I've ever come across is Scripture in Song by David and Dale Garratt. It's music of the 60s and 70s but this New Zealand couple led the early charismatic movement in the 70s and 80s in song and scripture memory with their contemporary music style. It was a wonderful way of learning inspirational memory verses.

Pray daily: This is one of the areas where some of us, as parents, have fallen down badly. Jesus' disciples were not used to praying. They had been brought up under the Old Testament system of worship where the priest was the one to access God. Individual worshippers usually didn't talk to God because they knew that the Aaronic priesthood had been put in place to teach them how to access God: through the priest. So, when Jesus' disciples saw Him praying, they said to Him, *"Lord, teach us to pray as John taught his disciples"* (Luke 11:1).

The Lord's prayer is not so much a prayer that is to be read out to God but a model teaching us how to approach God (i.e. in relationship) and then in what to ask for. Children can be taught this prayer and, as they get older, we can demonstrate how to use the model as a way to expand our prayers to Jesus. Preschool children often begin to pray by saying "Dear God, please bless Mummy, Daddy, my sister, Nan and Pop, the dog, the bird, the bus driver, and Mrs Johnson down the road. Amen." God loves to hear these simple prayers spoken from the heart of a child.

Eventually, their prayers can become more meaningful. When my daughter was two years old, she developed an allergy to our cat, Pippy, causing her to have hives between her elbow and wrist. We prayed for the healing of her allergy and she went off to play. About two hours later, she came to us to show us her arms. There were no more hives. She said, "Look Mum, my Pippy spots are gone!". We taught her to say thank you to Jesus for her healing.

Even to this day, as the mother of children herself, she is firm in her believe that Jesus heals!

Parenting Styles

In the western world, there are four types of parenting styles:

Authoritarian: strict with discipline; no negotiation; punishment for wrongdoing; top-down communication (from parent to child); high expectations; low flexibility. Taken to its extremes, this parenting style can be very controlling and abusive.

Permissive: Limited guidance and direction; no rules; children do their own problem-solving; open, but direction-less, communication; low expectations; high flexibility. This parenting style fails to provide children with a sense of trust or personal boundaries.

Uninvolved: freedom of actions; limited communication; limited nurturing, often from a lack of knowledge but sometimes from a lack of care; low expectations. Taken to its extremes, this parenting style can be neglectful and abusive.

Relational: reasonable expectations, clearly communicated; fosters self-discipline and creative thinking; well thought out reasons for discipline; age-related communication; nurturing; flexible; may have children's input where appropriate. There are no extremes with this parenting style. It produces well-balanced and mature children.

We can see from the above four parenting styles that the fourth one, Relational, provides for a better framework for discipleship. It imitates and models the Fathering nature of God with us. We pray *"Our Father who art in heaven..."* because that's how the Father wants us to relate to Him (Matthew 6:9). But it's not as easy as just choosing one style. Our own background and how our parents trained us will have a huge bearing on the style we follow. It's very easy to have the same style in raising our children as the one that was used on us. Not quite so easy, but just as common, is to react against the style used on us and choose a different style—generally, what we see as the complete opposite. But if we are intentionally training our children as disciples to Jesus we will think more clearly about our responsibility as a parent. We will *"train up a child in the way he should go..."* (Proverbs 22:6).

So, what is a reasonable expectation? It is outside the scope of this book to provide a detailed, age-related, how-to for all of our parenting needs. I'm more interested in providing practical tips on how to incorporate discipleship in our parenting. I would encourage you to use the research list at the end of this book. While I have provided some resources, they are only intended to be used as a starting point. The Developmental Milestones Chart, developed by the Institute for Human Services for the Ohio Child

Welfare Training Program, provides a wonderful framework for what you can expect of your child physically, cognitively, socially and emotionally for every age level from newborn up to adolescence.

Clear Communications

But a word on clear communication: I hear many parents asking their young children if they would like to do such and such. I cringe every time I hear that. "Would you like to clean up your bedroom now?" What child actually wants to clean up the bedroom? Or something that's worse: "Do you want a smack?" Can you imagine a child saying "Yes, please, mum!"?

Think again of the Training Event in the Chapter 2 Discipleship. We are the parent. We are training our child in a particular behaviour. We decide when they clean up their room, not them! If they are little, we will probably want to help. Remember, children learn best through play, so we make a game of it and we give praise for a job well done, even if we did more than half!

Young children can be quite literal in their understanding. If we say, "Would you like something to eat?", we have just provided the freedom for them to say, "Can I have some ice cream?". If we had thought more clearly, I'm sure we would have meant to say, "What would you like on your sandwich for lunch?" or for an older child who has learned the responsibility of cleaning the bedroom, we may say, "Would you like lunch now or after your bedroom is clean?".

How many times have you heard a parent say, "Stop that!"? You'll have to pardon the child for feeling a bit confused. They will be thinking "Stop what? — Playing with my Lego? Hitting my sister? Getting back my Lego man that she took from me? What?". The inappropriate behaviour needs to be described so that the child is in no doubt what you want them to do or stop doing. If the inappropriate behaviour is not clearly described, they won't know what or how to change.

Giving clear instructions can be quite a skill. We can learn from our own recipe books. Have you ever noticed that, when reading a set of procedures, each step usually begins with a doing word—mix, prepare, whip, and so forth. These words tell us clearly what we're meant to do. Our instructions need to be the same. Here is a possible communication between parent and child. See if you can see some of the pitfalls.

SCENARIO: 3-year-old is helping mum in the kitchen to cook a cake.

MUM: "Put that in there"

CHILD: "This?"

MUM: "Yes, that."

CHILD: "What?"

MUM: "That!" with a rising frustration.

Child puts a cup of flour in the bowl and the flour puffs up everywhere and goes all over the bench.

MUM: "Nooo. Not like that. Now I'll have to clean it up."

Child begins to wipe the flour off the bench into his hands, just like he's seen Mum do, but his hands are, by far, too small for the job.

MUM: "No! I told you to leave it! You're making a mess. Go and play. I'll finish this job by myself."

Does this go on in your house? This was a typical activity in my house until I learned about giving clear instructions. My poor children, who looked forward to cooking with Mum, went away unhappy and dejected. The worst part was that they didn't even know what they had done wrong!

Let's have a look at our scenario.

MUM: "Put that in there"

First of all, what is *"that"*? And where is *"there"*? Mum needed to say: "Gently put your cup of flour into the bowl but be careful. We don't want flour all over the bench"

CHILD: "This?"

Mum needed to say: "Yes, your cup of flour".

MUM: "Yes, that."

CHILD: "What?"

Again, with the *"that"* and *"what"*. Children need to learn to label items so that their language skills develop. This not only helps with procedural communication, but it also helps a child develop a good vocabulary.

MUM: "That!" with a rising temper.

Temper, temper Mum!

Child puts a cup of flour in the bowl and the flour puffs up everywhere and goes all over the bench.
This would be a good time to laugh! You might respond with *"Silly goose"*—and a floury touch on the nose. *"Don't worry. We'll clean up the mess later"*. Our child would not have been made to feel as if they had done something wrong, and the relationship between Mum and child is not impaired.

MUM: "Nooo. Not like that. Now I'll have to clean it up."

Mum's frustration is evident and the child, by now, is starting to feel insecure. They know they have displeased Mom but not why or how.

Child begins to wipe the flour off the bench into his hands, just like he's seen Mum do, but his hands are, by far, too small for the job.

MUM: "No! I told you to leave it! You're making a mess. Go and play. I'll finish this job by myself."

First of all, Mum didn't say to leave it, and what began as a fun activity together has now turned into a "job". When the time comes for cleaning up, it can be done together. The child can wipe the excess flour into Mum's hand (which is bigger) and still be doing something together. Then, Mum needs to say *"Good job. You were excellent at … [insert task]. We had fun, didn't we?"*.

In Matthew 25 and Luke 19, we have the parable of the talents. Jesus reports that the master was able to say "Well done". We may overlook the importance and the power of praise with our children in the busy-ness of everyday life. But Jesus taught the importance of praise in this simple parable.

We have looked at boundaries, choice and consequences and how these simple concepts can bring our children into greater maturity. We have also looked at different parenting styles and how to give clear communication to our children to help develop a Relationship style of parenting.

Within this Relationship style, we will look at how to correct inappropriate behaviour in our next chapter because, let's face it, with the best and clearest communication in the world, our children will still learn about the world around through making an unsatisfactory choice. What do we do then?

Correcting Inappropriate Behaviour

> ***Proverbs 29:15*** *"The rod and reproof give wisdom, but a boy let loose causes shame to his mother". LITV*

In this chapter we will cover…

- The Role of the Mother

- A brief look at separating inappropriate behaviour from behavioural issues

- Who sets the standard of behaviour for our family?

- The meaning behind commonly used words and how they affect the Training Journey

- Checking in-puts and through-puts in the Training Event

- The importance of restoration in correcting behaviour

- The 4-Rs of Correction

The Role of Parents in Setting Standards

Have you ever wondered why Proverbs 29:15 says shame is felt by the mother and not the father? I wondered for many years, until I learned that the training of children in a Jewish home was largely the responsibility of the mother. When they are older, they are then in their father's care, at which point they have learned the basic disciplines of life. The point at which there is a cross-over from Mum to Dad is at the Bar Mitzvah. According to www.Chabad.org, "*bar mitzvah*" is Hebrew for "*son of commandment*".

When a Jewish boy turns 13, he has all the rights and obligations of a Jewish adult. This is a practice that dates back over 3000 years, so Jesus would have participated in this ceremony.

The father takes over the son's education from this point on, but he is no longer considered a child but a man—a son of the commandment. So, there is no room for the father to feel shame; the basic life training of the child has already done by the mother. In the home, her word is law!

In our modern, western cultures the parenting duties fall to both parents. So, it's a bit hard to place shame (or guilt) on one parent alone. And our little cherubs seem to cotton on to this at any early age. They learn that, if Dad says NO, they might have a better chance with Mom.

Before we look at what "appropriate behaviour" is, and how to correct "inappropriate behaviour", we need to have a brief look at the increasingly prevalent incidence of learning and behavioural issues in our modern, western culture.

When my children were very young, I had a neighbour with an extremely "naughty" child. She tried to hide what was going on in her home, because she was under tremendous strain from the shame that was placed on her—both real and perceived. Some mothers in the neighbourhood really did look down on her for her inability to control her "naughty" child. And then there was the shame that she put on herself; she knew she couldn't cope, didn't have any answers, and didn't have any energy left to continue trying. She just felt like a failure.

As I developed a friendship with her, she allowed me into her home where I was able to see the behaviour of her child firsthand. He was about six years old when I first met him. He was totally non-complaint, threw tantrums often, and was physically violent with both Mum and his younger brother. Eventually, the mother confided to me that he had Attention Deficit Disorder (ADD). I must admit, I thought his "disorder" was of a different kind but, as I got to know them, I also learned more about the disorder. She had his bedroom window nailed shut and she had a lock on his door, but he was still able to get out of the house at night and play in the street! She lived opposite our local doctor, so he was also able to see the behaviour and prescribe some medication for him, which improved things for the mother, but still left the child with a problem.

By the time he was around ten years old, he began to understand that he was different. He realised that most people went to bed at night and slept for around eight hours, whereas he slept for around two hours each night, if he slept at all. As his brain developed and his understanding of other people grew, he was able to talk things through and to commit to staying in his bedroom, with the light on, playing with his toys and not going outside. There may have been other factors that exacerbated this problem, but, for the purpose of this book, we will only look at the ADD.

I am now involved with parents of children who have autism, dyslexia, dyspraxia, and a range of other learning behaviours. These parents have been labeled as "bad parents" by other school mums who don't seem to have a clue. We can be so judgemental of others. God forgive us for our wrong attitudes and our lack of support for those who rely us.

Training in Righteousness

We are the ones who decide what behaviour is appropriate for our children and no-one else! Now let me explain that statement. If we are raising disciples to Jesus, our standard of behaviour is already set out for us in passages such as *"Be imitators of God as dear children. And walk in love"* (Ephesians 5:1-2a); *"…nothing through selfish ambition or conceit, but in lowliness of mind let each esteem others better than himself"* (Philippians 2:3); *"Finally, brethren, whatever things are true…noble…just… pure…lovely…of good report…meditate on these things"* (Philippians 4:8); *"… put on tender mercies, kindness, humility, meekness, long-suffering, bearing with one another, if anyone has a complaint against another, even as Christ forgave you, so you also…Let the word of Christ dwell in you richly in all wisdom, teaching and admonishing one another in psalms and hymns and spiritual songs, singing with grace in your hearts to the Lord"* (Colossians

3:12-13, 16); Colossians 3:18-4:6; Ephesians 6:1-9 and many more.

As we encounter these passages, the Spirit of the Living God will quicken our hearts with revelation and enable us, by His grace, to walk in them ourselves and to impart them to our children. We can't train others in what we are not walking in ourselves. We, also, can't grit our teeth and try really, really hard to *"imitate Christ"*. We need His grace to be our enabling power. That's what grace is: *The Presence of the Spirit of God within us to enable to do what He has called us to do.* When I was a young Christian, I learned that grace was **G**od's **R**iches **A**t **C**hrist's **E**xpense but I now find that that is an empty, platitudinous statement that doesn't really give us any understanding.

I have also heard Christians refer to the grace of God as being the opposite of law. That is not a good description, either, because the opposite of law is lawlessness—not grace!

If we refer back to the Training Event in Chapter 2 Discipleship, we see that Point A, Current Behaviour, is the behaviour that our children are currently displaying and that Point B, Desired Behaviour, is the current revelation we have received from the Spirit. The Training Process is then the journey we go on, as a family, to conform ourselves to the will of God as presented to us in His Word. This is the "appropriate behaviour".

What do we do, then, for inappropriate behaviour? Let's review 'correction', 'discipline' and 'punishment', then establish definitions for other words that often lead us into 'the sea of confusion' so that we are speaking a consistent language.

Punishment: the affliction of a penalty as retribution for an offence. Even the language of this definition tells us that punishment is negative—affliction, penalty, retribution, offence. When we offer punishment, there is no love of Christ. Deuteronomy 32:35a says vengeance and retribution belong to Him so if we offer punishment, we are actually stepping into God's shoes and doing His job for Him. As if we could!

Correction: a change that rectifies an error or inaccuracy. Referring again to the Training Event, the Training Process can be thought of as "a pathway to get from Point A to Point B". As our children are learning to walk on that pathway, we give feedback to let them know how they're doing; we give encouragement to help them keep going; we give praise for a job well done; and, we give correction for when they begin to stray off that pathway. The whole point of training is to *"change behaviour"* so we need to gently guide them along that pathway.

Discipline: the practice of following a set of rules or behaviours. Discipline can be externally motivated, especially when our children are at the beginning of the pathway of learning, but we hope as parents and trainers, that the motivation will become internalised, that is, they will see the value of the rule or behaviour and want to adopt it for themselves.

Consequences: the result or effect of a certain action, belief or choice. Consequences can be positive or negative.

Rights: are entitlements owed to us or other people. Different cultures see rights quite differently but in the modern, western nations they are often enshrined in law. Great social upheaval is taking place, now, as a result of minority factions lobbying for social change. Without making comment on specific "rights", it doesn't take too much observation to see that "rights" can often be misunderstood.

In the realm of Human Resources, many employers have written into their awards a "provision" for sick leave. Many workers see those allocated days as a "right" and don't understand the difference between a provision and a right. Media influence on our teens and children is also giving them the idea that they have certain "rights" as a child, such as the right to have a mobile phone in the classroom. What they don't understand is that rights come with inherent "responsibilities".

Responsibilities: a duty to steward the things under our control. Examples of where we have responsibilities might include:

- Body: being responsible for personal space and physical touch
- Mind: being responsible for our thoughts, feelings and attitudes, and respecting those who are different
- Emotions: being responsible for displaying or limiting our emotions

- Sexuality: being responsible for bodily desires, accepting them as a God-given blessing

- Possessions: being responsible for the condition and maintenance of toys, money and other possessions

- Time: being responsible for how we spend the 24 hours of each day and what we accomplish

Privileges: a special advantage or reward earned for conformance to certain behaviours. Children need to learn that responsibilities are due before a privilege can be earned. One of the things taught in the parable of the talents is just this: when the different stewards achieved a certain result, a reward, or privilege was given. The greater the result, the greater the reward (Matthew 25:14-29).

Correction in Training

Now we're almost already to talk about correcting inappropriate behaviour. We have received the revelation, communicated the standard, demonstrated the behaviour and given feedback along the way. Then, for some inexplicable reason, our little angel goes off track. We have to ask ourselves a few questions:

- Am I remiss in any way? Did I receive a revelation that can be backed up by the Word of God?

- Did I communicate the standard in clear, direct and easy-to-understand language?

- Am I demonstrating the required behaviour or am I expecting my child to do what I am not yet doing?

- Have I broken the learning steps down into bite-size pieces or have I expected too much?

- Is there any attitude, or anything I have done, that would cause this inappropriate behaviour?

In other words, "Was any of my behaviour 'inappropriate'?"

The Purpose of Correction

The primary purpose of correction is to bring us back to a right relationship with God. If we endeavor to bring our children back to our heavenly Father, in correction, we need to make sure we have not contributed to their inappropriate "output", or behavior. We need to check our "inputs" and our "throughputs". This is not an exercise in "blaming the mother". This is making sure that we separate our behaviour from that of our child. When we can stand before our Father and have Him say that we are blameless, we can then deal with the inappropriate behaviour.

Notice that I am not calling it "bad" behaviour. When evaluating any training event, it is customary to look at inputs (what goes into the training event), outputs (the end result) and through-puts (what happens in the training process). By asking those questions of ourselves, we have looked at the inputs and, to some extent, the through-puts.

The inputs are what we put into the training: our understanding of the revelation from the Spirit, and our understanding of the Word (Was our understanding backed up by other scriptures? Was it in context? and so on). Then we look at our part of the through-put: our communication, our training steps and our attitude during the process.

Our best "standard" in evaluating our training is the Holy Spirit. We take the inappropriate behaviour to the Father and ask Him to reveal to us, by His Spirit, if we have contributed toward the inappropriate behaviour. When we are satisfied that, either we have dealt with anything that was remiss on our part, or we are not culpable, we can move on. I know a mother who used to say to her children, when they were naughty, "That's it! I'm going to talk to God." And she would go into her bedroom to pray.

Looking back, her adult daughter said that she would know, when Mum did this, that her behaviour had gone too far and things were very serious. She would say to her Mum "No, Mum. Don't talk to God. I'll be good."

When she looks back, she laughs but she also knows that her mother modeled a very effective behaviour for her: to talk to God about her children whenever she was feeling overwhelmed or needed to check her inputs and through-puts.

If the Father shows us any inappropriate behaviour in use, we need to deal with it simply and quickly through repentance and confession so we can get on with the job of correcting our children's inappropriate behaviour.

Correction and Restoration

Sin separates us from God. Romans 3:23 tells us **"all have sinned and fall short of the glory of God"**. *Sin separates us from* God's glory. The original Greek word has the idea of *missing the mark* as if an arrow was missing the target. The target is the glory of God.

God has always intended for us to live in His glory, but mankind was separated from His glory when we were sent out of the garden, out of His Presence. This was the result of sin. But, through Jesus, we now have a way back into His Presence, back into the glory. When correcting inappropriate behaviour, the goal is restoration of His Presence. The goal of correction is always restoration.

Correction is for restoration. Galatians 6:1 tell us that, if a man (person, child) is overtaken in a fault, we are to restore them in the spirit of meekness. With my own children, my husband and I used spanking as a method of correction. We had both come from broken families and so we had no effective model of parenting to follow. We had been taught by other people in the church that Proverbs 22:15 taught that all children were born naughty and that we should use *"the rod of correction"* which, of course, was a spanking.

But when we fostered children through the Department of Child Welfare, we were not allowed, by law, to spank so we had to come up with another method of correction that would be effective. Before we get into a debate about spanking, I want to show you the revelation that I received from God.

In the first week of these two foster girls coming to stay with us, they weren't game to misbehave. In the second week, however, they began to feel more comfortable with us and the older girl, who was around nine or ten years old and was used to protecting her younger siblings, decided to challenge me when I issued a directive. Initially, I was surprised and didn't know how to respond. Almost instinctively, I said 1…—, 2…—, and waited for a response. Just as I was about to say—3, she decided not to push the issue, and did what I ask her to do. After she had gone, I realised that if I had gotten to 3 and she still had not obeyed, I wouldn't have had a clue what to do next! That incident sent me into the prayer closet!

In the Prayer Closet

The revelation I received on correcting inappropriate behaviour came in two parts. The second part of the revelation was concerning *"the rod of correction"*. The original Greek word for "rod" in Proverbs is *shebet* which means *"a stick (for punishing, writing, fighting, ruling, walking)"*.

Proverbs uses the meaning almost exclusively for punishing. But Jeremiah 51:19 uses the same words and talks of *"the rod of his inheritance"* and says, *"Jehovah of Hosts is His name"*.

I found that very interesting. Jehovah of Hosts is another name for God. Jeremiah is calling God *"the rod"*! Then in Ezekiel 20, God is talking to Israel about restoration and is telling them that he will *"cause them to pass under the rod"*. Isaiah calls it the *"rod of His mouth"* in chapter 11. So, it seems, that when we take all that the Word has to say on the subject of the rod, it is not just for punishment, but for correction, or for re-establishing according to a standard. The standard (of our behaviour) is God, manifest as Jesus in the flesh, and *"passing under the rod"* is a euphemism for being judged according to the standard of behaviour set by Jesus, firstly when He was on the earth and, secondly as recorded in His Word, the Bible. I realise I have made some bold statements here, but I don't want to spend too much space on Bible study. If you feel inclined and want or need more information, study the word "rod" for yourselves. As I said, this was my revelation.

My first revelation came in answer to my prayer when I used the 1-2-3 technique with my foster children (I'll explain this a bit later on). God showed me, first, three parts to correcting inappropriate behaviour and then added a fourth when I was praising and thanking Him for the revelation, and how well it had worked when I put it into practice. So here is my revelation: "The 4-Rs of Wrongdoing":

1. Recognition: *All we like sheep have gone astray; we have each one turned to his own way; and Jehovah made meet in Him the iniquity of all of us" Isaiah 53:6 (LITV).*

This may seem like a "no brainer", but our children need to admit that they have done something wrong. This teaches them humility and dependence on God's righteousness. They may also need to be coached in exactly what was the inappropriate behaviour. Our instructions for appropriate behaviour need to be clear and understood, regardless of the age of the child; in the same way, our description of what was not acceptable needs to be in clear, easy-to-understand and age-appropriate language.

One of my foster girls used to pick up loose change in the school playground. Some of the children came from extremely wealthy families and were given notes of large denominations for buying food at school. They were apathetic about caring for the change that was given to them from the Tuckshop and used to throw the coins on the ground. School policy was that any money found at school was to be handed in at the Office. If it wasn't claimed by the end of term, the person handing in the money was allowed to keep it.

I tried to explain that this was the behaviour I expected but my foster child couldn't see anything wrong with capitalising on someone else's apathy. We went through the "school rules" routine, the "stealing if it's not yours" and a few other minor routines, but she just couldn't get it.

Eventually, I had to let it drop, — but I prayed about it. Eventually, circumstances conspired against her. She "lost" something through a lack of diligence and a friend picked it up. She tried to claim ownership, and I was on hand at the time, so I was able to show her how someone else was now acting on her principles (or lack of) and she was suffering as a result. She finally got it and from then on, she could understand her inappropriate actions when we needed to talk them through.

2. Repentance: *"Repent and be baptized for the remission of sins" Acts 2:38*

This step involves changing the mind and turning around. I usually demonstrate this with a whole-body movement. I walk in one direction and talk as I'm going, explaining that my current behaviour is taking me in this direction in life, as a downward path; then I gently hit my forehead with the palm of my hand, say "Oh. I need to change my mind. This behaviour (naming it) is wrong"; spin around 180 degrees, heading in the opposite direction, saying "Now that I've changed my mind, I'm taking my life in the direction of Jesus". This usually demonstrates the dual action of changing my mind and turning around so that I go in a different direction. This is repentance. Anything less than this is just "being sorry" and it could be that I'm sorry I got caught, or I'm sorry this time, but I'll probably do it again. But there is also another aspect to repentance which involves forgiveness. It is the complete removal of the chains that have bound us to the action for which we have just repented. That is why God says, in 1 John 1:9, that *"if we confess our sins He is faithful and just to forgive our sins **and to cleanse us from all unrighteousness"*** (emaphasis mine).

3. Restitution: *"and hearing this, they were cut to the heart and said...'What must we do?'" Acts 2:37*

Restitution is about correcting the wrong I did. If my child broke a glass because they were playing around and not being careful, especially after being warned, they need to replace the glass by purchasing a new one. If it is one of a set and can't be replaced, they need to use their pocket money to cover the cost of its original purchase or do a job that is sufficient to make up for it. If they broke the glass as they were wiping it up and they dropped it because it was too soapy, then it was an accident, and they don't need to pay for it. Accidents happen! If correction is for restoration, then we need to ask ourselves "What am I restoring?". Sometimes it will be a relationship. Sometimes it will be someone's prized possession. There will always be something that needs to be restored.

4. Reconciliation: *"If we confess our sin, He is Faithful and Just to forgive us our sin and to cleanse us from all unrighteousness." 1 John 1:9 "Our Father, who is in heaven" Matthew 6:9*

We need to make sure we bring our child back into fellowship with us and with God. This demonstrates the merciful, forgiving nature of our Father, Himself. When we are sure that our child has recognised their inappropriate behaviour, truly repented, and made restitution as appropriate, we can now lead them in reconciliation.

This begins with saying "sorry" to the aggrieved person. It is not just "Sorry". It is "I'm sorry for (and name the behaviour)". The naming of the inappropriate behaviour promotes humility. It is at this stage that we can tell if our child has truly repented. If there is a reluctance to name the inappropriate behaviour, we can be sure that there is no true repentance. If there is a reluctance to make reconciliation to a person, this can be seen in a lack of willingness to make eye contact, a tone in the voice that says, "I am a victim here", and so on.

Next, the aggrieved person says, "I forgive you" and gives our child a cuddle. It's amazing how a cuddle can quickly restore a broken relationship. When we say sorry to God, we may need to lead our little one in the prayer until they are old enough to understand what they are doing and how prayer works.

One last thing on correcting inappropriate behaviour… Have you ever wondered why or how the principle of a school has so much authority? To some extent, the authority is built into the position. But as well as that, the personal authority of the principal has been growing throughout their career. As a newly graduated student, the novice teacher must learn how to put into practice the class management techniques that were learnt during formal studies. They learn that one particular technique may not work on a windy day, or with a particular student. They learn what works and what doesn't work. Over time, students learn to recognise the authority of the teacher.

The teacher's authority has been building and growing. Some teachers seem to wear authority like a cloak. There are some teachers that students know not to cross—or else!

In the same way, parents develop their authority over time. We begin with a gorgeous little baby who can do no wrong. They are a delight in every way. We wake up one morning and we have a toddler on our hands! We begin to exercise authority in small steps for us and the child. Over time, we build up our authority and our set of acceptable behaviours as our children learn to recognise the authority that has been growing in their parents. Not that they are aware of our growing authority—they just think that Mum and Dad know, and can do, everything.

I believe Jesus has designed our families this way to teach us how to develop spiritual authority. Did you know that God intends the church to make known, to principalities and powers in the heavenly places, the many-sided wisdom of God, according to Ephesians 3:10? And according to Ephesians 2:6, *"we have been raised together with Christ Jesus"*, and we are sitting *"together in heavenly places"* with Him. This is obviously not to be taken literally, at least not yet. The meaning behind this verse is that, if we are sitting with him in those heavenly places, we are sitting in the place of authority in His name—the place of rulership, the place where a King or Queen would sit.

Have you ever noticed that "Parliament is sitting", or that "the Queen is sitting"? That doesn't mean they are physically on a chair, or throne, but that they are in a place where they have assumed the role of rulership, a place where they are able and ready to make laws and decrees—as distinct from when they were on holidays. God wants us to rule and to reign, in His name, here on earth. This is the essence of spiritual authority. *"First the natural, then the spiritual"* (1 Corinthians 15:46). We learn that natural authority in the home and then, as we grow and develop in prayer for our children, we learn and develop spiritual authority.

In this chapter, we have looked at the wonderful role of the mother in the family and how we need to be aware of some behavioural issues that may arise with children. As the parents set the standard of behaviour for the family, we need to make sure we have a consistent understanding of commonly used words so that our standards are the same. If we have contributed to inappropriate behaviour, we have looked at how to handle this before we embark on the corrective action needed to bring restoration. Lastly, we have discovered the 4Rs of the corrective process. Next, we will look at a Biblical model of discipleship and how to use this model to lead our children into a greater walk toward maturity in Jesus.

Beyond Foundations

Hebrews 5:14 *"And this we will do, if God permits."* LITV

In this chapter we will cover…

- Corporate and personal foundations for building lives
- Partnering with Jesus to do the building
- Eight clear steps in making disciples
- Practical teaching on money management and emotional self-control
- The six foundations of the faith and how to impart them
- Right relationships for husbands, wives and children

Foundations

Jesus used the analogy of a building to describe our journey into maturity. He is the foundation upon which the building is built. If a house doesn't have strong foundations, it won't stand. As the *"Apostle and High Priest of our profession"* (Hebrews 3:1), He is the Master Apostle that is building the church of God (His house) (2 Corinthians 5:1). This is an eternal house.

This is a corporate house as well as an individual house (Hebrews 3:6). In Hebrews 10:21, we see that Jesus is THE *"High Priest over the house of God"* (the church). This house is called *"a house of prayer"* (in Matthew 21:13), as a corporate house. And in 1 Peter 2:5, we are described as *"lively stones"* (some of us are livelier than others!), *"a spiritual house"*, as an individual house.

We know that every house needs a strong foundation. The parable of Matthew 7 tells us what happens to a house when it is not built on a strong foundation. The Apostle Paul tells us, in 1 Corinthians 3:10-11, as *"a wise master builder"*, that he is *"laying a foundation"* for this corporate house of God and that his work is laid upon the foundation rock that is Jesus. He also brings a caution to us here. Be careful how you build! Take heed how you build—look at what you are doing. This caution is not designed to make us fear what we are doing, or to fear retribution from God. Our God is not that kind of God; He is not a capricious God who delights in finding us doing something wrong! To *"take heed"* really means to look at what we are doing; to be purposeful in the building so that we will take pleasure in the final structure—the lives of our children, in this case.

I was very heartened at one time, when I was doubting my ability to be a good parent, by seeing a funny quip on the internet. It said, with an appropriate picture of Adam, Eve and the apple, "If God couldn't look after His children, what makes you think you can do better?". Obviously, that was a tongue-in-cheek comment, but there is also an element of truth. We are not infallible! That is a very sobering reflection.

But God is our Father and He understands our pain, our short-comings and our heart's motivations. He longs for us to come to Him in humility and to say "I can't do this; can You help me, please?". No-one has ever done the job of raising this child before! Sure, lots of people have raised children before, but not your particular child! God has entrusted that stewardship to you because He thinks you are the best person to do the job, with the aid of His Spirit.

Partnering with Jesus

We are building into our children's lives. We are partnering with Jesus, as the apostle Paul was, to build them as an individual, and as part of a corporate, too does that also form part of our training in God. We are trained by the Word and the Spirit of God; we train our children to be trained by the Word and Spirit of God.

We begin our training as a novice — a "newbie"; our little cherubs, who can do no wrong in our eyes, also begin their training as novices. There is an old saying: "When a child is born, a father is born". This applies to mothers as well, and so the journey begins together; babes learn to grow and develop, going through many stages of accomplishment; parents learn to grow and develop as parents, leaders, protectors, educators, spiritual mentors, and so on. It takes time, commitment and discipline to implement the Training Event in the life of a child but, when you get to be an adult and you can stand side-by-side with your child to worship Jesus, or even go on missionary trips together, there is no greater joy!

We begin our stewardship as a parent by implementing such things as prayer, reading about Jesus, boundaries, respect for others, manners, and following instructions. These simple activities help us to create in our children a *"pure heart"* (Psalm 24:4) which will guide them into discipleship.

Making Disciples

Making disciples, according to the imperative command of Matthew 28:19-20, begins with eight very clear steps:

Preach the gospel (Mark 16:15). What is the gospel? If we are to preach it to our children, we need to know what it is. There are whole books on this subject alone, so just a summary is required here.

Firstly, we need to understand what the gospel is NOT; it is not just believing in God so we can go to heaven. That belief short-changes us of so much that the Father has in store for us. The book of Ephesians is wonderful for showing us what God has in store for those who believe. Chapter 1 tells us about the church's position in Jesus: we have been blessed with every spiritual blessing in heavenly places! How awesome! Two of those blessings include the *"Spirit of Wisdom"* and the *"Spirit of Revelation"* (verse 17).

We don't have to do it on our own. Whatever situation we are facing, we can do it with the wisdom of His Spirit and the revelation of His Word. Chapter 2 tells us we are seated with Jesus in heavenly places, in a place of spiritual authority! Again, how awesome! We can rule over those dark forces that seek to come against us and our children. We have a natural, in-built, God-given instinct to protect our young.

As a Christian walking in the Spirit, we have been given the authority to be successful. Chapter 3 then tells us that the purpose of chapters 2 and 3 is so that the church can be a demonstration of God's wisdom and power.

Chapter 4 tells us that walking in the Spirit is to walk in unity, love and wisdom, being obedient as children, parents and employees — and then, we are sufficiently trained to engage in spiritual warfare. We not only preach this gospel in simple, easy-to-understand language with our children, but we also demonstrate it through the way we are living. The *"gospel"* is the *"good news of the kingdom"*. It is a new realm of divine activity here on earth. It is the place where there an all-sufficient, loving, powerful Father-King ruling and reigning in complete autonomy.

Baptise into the Name of the Father, Son and Holy Spirit (Mark 16:16). Galatians 2:20 says *"we have been crucified with Christ"* and Romans 6:4 says we were *"buried with Him in baptism"*. I have not found anywhere in the Word of God where it says that baptism is "an outward sign of an internal change".

I heard that as a young believer but, thanks to God, I found these two passages that say that I was actually crucified and buried. Now, I don't understand the unseen workings of the doctrine but neither do I understand the workings of the combustion engine; I just have faith that, when I turn the key in the ignition of my car, something under the bonnet happens and the car works. Baptism is the same; by faith in Jesus, the Christ (the Anointed One), when I was baptised, something in the spirit world happened and baptism worked (in putting to death the *"old man"* of Romans 6:6). Now I know, beyond a shadow of a doubt, that I have the power to overcome resident within me as I access the Spirit of the Living God, who also resides in me.

Teach them to observe all things (2 Timothy 2:15). What are the *"all things"*? We have already covered some of the basics of training a child. As this book is not, primarily, a book on raising children, it can't cover all that we need to know as parents. This book's focus is on raising disciples in the home, to follow Jesus; to be a *"learner"* of Jesus; to follow you as you are an example of the life of a disciple (2 Thessalonians 3:9). *"For you were called to this…that you should follow in His steps"* (1 Peter 2:21). So, we begin with the foundations of our faith, Hebrews 6:1-3, and God will issue a (building) permit for us and our children to grow in maturity. We also teach them to:

- be devoted to Jesus in *prayer* (Luke 18:1)

- read the *Bible* as the Word of God to us and them, reading for understanding, study and meditation (Psalm 119:105, 2 Timothy 3:16)

- live in *fellowship*, doing acts of service, learning how to relate, learning how to take correction, enjoying each other's company, demonstrating love for each other (Acts 2:44-47)

- *minister* in fellowship as we attend church or home group, ministering in service and the Word as we are graced by God (1 Peter 4:10-11)

- *steward* resources, such as toys, money, natural giftings (Matthew 25:14-29)

- *submit* to authority, as to the Lord, and trust those who shepherd them—in the home, the church and society (Hebrews 13:17), *"praying for all men everywhere"* (1 Timothy 2:1)

- be prepared to be *"sent"* as a worker in God's harvest, not focusing on personal desires (Luke 10:2)

Continue steadfastly (Acts 2:42). We can't give up when things are difficult — as they surely will be at some stage. The rains will come, without a doubt, but are we the ones whose lives are built firmly on the solid rock? When the storms of life come (such as having to face a bully at school), do we teach our children to cry out to God? Do we throw out our *"anchor"* (Hebrews 6:19) and expect it to land in something solid?

I always thought, as I grew up in my teenage years, that it was the anchor which saved me—not knowing anything about the art of sailing. The anchor, which represents our faith, is important in stopping the boat from drifting but it is actually what the anchor is embedded in to (which is Jesus) that saves us. If we throw out our anchor and it lands in the golden sands of our tropical beaches, there is not much substance there and the boat may not hold; but, if we throw out the anchor and it becomes embedded into rock (again, Jesus), we have a much better chance of staying put even in the wildest of storms. We need to teach our children, standing with them in prayer and encouragement, to continue in their faith even in the face of friends at school who don't believe and who may even criticise them for believing.

Breaking bread (Acts 2:42). This was a very clear teaching in the book of Acts. The disciples did it *"from house to house"* and *"daily"* (Acts 2:42,46). Some churches teach that, in order for us to have communion, we need to be led by a minister or priest. I can see no evidence for that in the Bible. In fact, it is the reverse. In the book of Revelations, Jesus tells the church at Ephesus that he hates the doctrine of the Nicolaitans (Revelation 2:6).

This doctrine teaches that there is a separation between the clergy (ministers) and laity (the ordinary people) and Jesus says it is wrong. Revelations 1:6 says that we are all (those who have had their sins washed by His blood) *"kings and priests to God"*. So, if it is true that we need a priest to serve the communion, we are all priests! The teaching on having communion begins with Exodus 12, where God gave the first instructions for the Passover—the pattern for Communion. This passage, from verse 1 to verse 28, gives instructions to celebrate Passover with a lamb (a pattern of Jesus' death), a grain offering (a pattern of Jesus' body) and the blood on the door posts (a pattern of Jesus' shed blood). Then in 1 Corinthians 11:23, the apostle Paul says he received the instructions for the celebration of the Lord's Supper *"from the Lord"*, using the bread and the cup (of wine).

The book of Hebrews was written as a warning to those early Christians, the majority of whom were Jewish, to not go back into Judaism but to stay in the new covenant blessing prophetically given in Jeremiah 31:31-34. In Hebrews 8, the writer of Hebrews is reminding the Christians of those blessings. He says in verse 7 that *"if the first* (covenant) *had been faultless, then no place would have been sought for a second"* (NKJV).

It has been my personal testimony that, as we celebrate Communion in our home on a daily basis, it has served as a weapon of our warfare. It is a visible reminder that we are covered by the blood of Jesus on a daily basis. My grandchildren are excited to have a meal with us and to "have the blood". As young as they are, they understand that Jesus paid something for them that they couldn't afford to pay. As they grow older, they also learn what that price is: *"You were bought with a price; then glorify God in your body, and in your spirit, which are of God"* 1 Corinthians 6:20).

Prayers (Matthew 6:9-13, 1 Timothy 2:8). There are whole books on this subject alone but, just as an introduction, we need to *"Watch! Be wakeful and pray…"* (Matthew 13:33). We need to practice *"asking, seeking, knocking"* (Matthew 7:7-8) in prayer; supplications (pleading) like the widow in Luke 18; intercession (on behalf of others) and the many other forms of prayer. We need to pray for our needs, the needs of others, the government as the authority over us. We need to sit still and practice the art of listening in our prayers. And this is what we teach our young disciples. We cannot teach what we don't walk in ourselves. We need to teach our children to have faith in a God who can answer us when we call (Psalm 86:7), move heaven and earth on our behalf (Matthew 17:20), and who walks before us as a consuming fire to devour all our enemies (Hebrews 12:29).

Walking in our inheritance What is our inheritance? Can we have it now, or do we need to wait until we get to heaven? The doctrine that teaches we get everything in heaven after we die is selling us short of what we can walk in NOW! We have been *"blessed with every spiritual blessing in the heavenliness with Christ"* (Ephesians 1:3); we are *"seated with Him in heavenly places"* (Ephesians 2:6) — which means that we are in the place of authority with Him, ruling and reigning over the affairs of mankind on His behalf; we have already (past tense) *"obtained an inheritance"* (Ephesians 1:11).

We are heirs of the promise of Abraham, if we are walking in Christ as a son, according to Galatians 3:29. This is present tense. It is something we should be walking in now, in the promises of God, in maturity.

My husband was working in a situation where his supervisor managed from the principle of "throw them in the deep end and, if they're any good they'll float; if not, throw them back"! He was an extremely critical and unkind boss to all in his team. We prayed for him for months, mostly for his salvation but also for his "softening".

Eventually, under the revelation of the Holy Spirit, we prayed that, if he was not going to come to salvation or to change in any way, that God would remove him from that position. Within three days, he had been given his notice and had left. Don't mess with a son of the Most High God! We have an inheritance to walk in, here and now!

As sons of God Our recognition that we are sons of Almighty God is linked to our walk in maturity! We don't really understand what a big deal this is for us until we understand about *"sonship"*. This word is used to describe our relationship with God. John 1:12 says we have been given the right, or authority, to be a child of God when we first believed. The Greek word that was used here is the word **teknon**. It is a generic word for child in an intimate and reciprocal relationship, but of no specified age.

But if we skip over to Galatians 4:1-7, where the apostle Paul talks about us being a **son** and **heir**, we see that there is a growing process. We start out as babes; in Greek it is the word **nepios**, meaning baby. We may be the heir of a super large fortune but, as a baby, we are not able to inherit. We have to grow up. We have to become a **huios** son. It is the *"Spirit of adoption"* (Romans 8:15) that we have received that energises, or motivates, us to cry out "Daddy, Father" to Almighty God (Romans 8:23). Jesus taught us to pray to *"our Father, in heaven"* in Matthew 6:9. He understood about adoption. In Luke 2:49, after Jesus had stayed behind in Jerusalem and was eventually found by His parents in the Temple, He said to them *"Didn't you know I must be about My Father's business?"*. He wasn't talking about His father, Joseph, He was talking about His Father, Almighty God. At the age of 12-13 Jewish boys, then and now, undergo a ceremony, a "bar mitzvah", during which they promise to no longer behave as a child but to be responsible for their own spiritual life and development. It was also at this time that the boys would no longer be under the care and instruction of their mother but would then go into the family business. This is what Jesus was referring to, but He also understood He was still under the guardianship of Mary and Joseph (Luke 2:51).

There is so much wonderful teaching on "sonship" available. One of the best resources I have seen is *"Walking in Our Inheritance"*, by apostle, Paul Galligan, available free from Revival Ministries Australia.

Practical Teaching on Emotional Control

A teacher always has more information than what they give out to the student. A parent is exactly the same. We can't expect our children to be able to receive all that we have. Their brains just aren't capable of receiving it all. That's why we have to give instruction in small, clear, and precise steps. Money management is a good example of this.

We can't teach our five-year-old the benefits of budgeting, but we can allow them to experience the joy of "pocket money". When we had our foster children, we gave them a certain amount of money, based on age, which they could do with as they chose.

They were all old enough to understand tithing (the giving of 10% of their money) so the only stipulation we had on their pocket money was that they had to tithe. They could choose where the tithe was paid to and one of our foster children chose to give it to charity, but the other gave it to the church we attended (which is the true tithe).

Even so, they both learned to be dependent on God for their finances and their income. It was interesting to see how they handled their money. Our five-year-old hadn't had anything to do with money in the past, so she just spent it. She was like a whirlwind when she went to the shops. If she had five cents left over, she would walk around the shops looking for something that cost five cents so she could buy it.

On the other hand, our ten-year-old had been used to having her biological mother "borrow" any money she received and not repay it; when she was given pocket money, she didn't spend one cent of it for over six months!

She just hoarded it. I had to encourage her to spend it and that was a hard job. You could see her financial insecurity on a weekly basis. However, as we taught our kids about money, their maturity developed over a period of time. They learned:

- we are all totally dependent on our Father for our income and our ability to earn it (that's partly why we tithe);
- to spend money and the joy that comes with having disposable income;
- to calculate change, using a quick mental process of approximation;
- to recognise "affordability", understanding why some families had a basic Holden and other families could afford a BMW;
- to choose wisely between alternatives — the cheapest item was not always the best use of money;
- the stewardship of possessions;
- the recognition of others' efforts and appreciation for gifts received;
- to regulate their desires for "things" — although this took longer to learn than all the other skills and values put together.

Some of these skills were transferred on to regulating their feelings. As they learned to regulate their money and possessions, they also learned to regulate their feelings.

First of all, they learned to recognise what they were feeling, and we could talk them through why they were feeling that way. Interestingly, the five-year-old was more in touch with her feelings and well able to articulate what she was feeling. The ten-year-old, who had been more psychologically affected by her biological mother, was less able to recognise what she was feeling, and this was manifested in anger. It took a lot longer to help her recognise her feelings but, once she did, she was able to regulate her emotions so that she displayed some measure of self-control.

Without a degree in psychology, or any other training, how did I know how to lead and guide them through the minefield of emotions? I look back and ask myself the same question. I can honestly say that having foster children threw me more into prayer than having my own children did. This was partly due to my increased maturity and partly due to the increased sense of responsibility I had for someone else's children.

I would talk to God about every issue we were facing with the children. This is how God showed me what I call "The 4-Rs of Wrongdoing" mentioned in Chapter 5. I would often receive a word of knowledge regarding the behaviour of those children.

In fact, one of the children said she didn't think that God liked her. When I asked her why, she said it was because He kept telling me (through the words of knowledge) what she was up to! Now, this sounds like a negative and, on the surface, it may well be but, when she is older, she will remember the power of the Spirit that was working through me for her benefit. I haven't lost hope for her!

Regulating money and emotions are just a part of the training we could be giving to older children. We could also be teaching them about having a healthy mind—regulating what they watch on all forms of electronic media and even the total amount of time spent on this media. We can teach them to have a love of books by reading to them and encouraging them to read for themselves, especially the "classics". When they have read—or had read to them—books such as *Charlotte's Web*, *Mary Poppins*, the *Narnia* series, we can then have a family night of watching the movie, along with pizza, chips, or whatever takes their fancy.

Our training should begin with foundations, both in the natural and the spiritual, and move on to more advanced concepts and skills, using the Training Event described in Chapter 2. We can then move on to training in leadership. On the way to leadership, we can teach them about the Foundations of the Faith in Hebrews 6.

Foundations of the Faith

When I was first asked what the foundations of my faith were, I answered, rather hesitatingly, "Um, prayer, Bible reading, arrh, love. Yes, definitely love. Love is important." and I had no idea that the Bible actually tells us what our foundations are.

Later on, I thought I should have said, "repentance for my sins" but, even then, I didn't have a very clear idea of what I was saying. When it was pointed out to me that Hebrews actually lists them, I realised I had been a baby Christian for over 35 years! Yes, I had led prayer teams, I had prayed for the impartation of the Holy Spirit, I had prophesied and led worship — but as far as the Word of God was concerned, I was a baby. I had, unknowingly, operated out of the laity/clergy divide by allocating the knowledge of the Word to those who were considered preachers and teachers, allowing them to instruct me in what I should believe.

I now recognise that, if I am to weather the storms of life spoken by Jesus in Matthew 7, having my spiritual house built upon a rock, then I need to know what the Rock says in every given situation I face. I need to know the Word for myself. I can testify that my prayer life is now so different to what it was before. I know how to pray the Word, how to declare the truth of God in prayer, how to overcome in prayer instead of always asking plaintively for God to do what He wants me to do — rule and reign in every situation through prayer and His other weapons of warfare.

So, let's look, briefly, at the six foundations listed in Hebrews:

1. Repentance from dead works: This covers all the sins of the flesh, the ones we committed before we came to faith in Jesus, as well as the works that we try to do for Him of which He has not graced us. Much of the training of our children may be in this foundation: A Biblical repentance from all the things that are *"bound in the heart of a child"* (Proverbs 22:15).

2. Faith toward God: Although it seems redundant to state that we need to have faith toward God, it is possible to be sorry for past sins and then to turn to Buddhism or some other religion. If we are to truly repent, this involves a turning away from our sins and a turning toward a different direction — a

180-degree turnaround, so these two foundations really are different sides of the same coin. This is the focus of our discipleship — faith toward God.

3. Doctrine of baptisms: Notice that it is in the plural. While there is only one baptism into *"the faith"*, according to Ephesians 4:5, there are several aspects to that baptism. Just briefly, there is baptism in water (Romans 6:3-14), baptism in the Spirit (Acts 1:5,8), and baptism into the body of Christ (Ephesians 4:4-6). When the time is right, when our little disciple demonstrates a sure willingness to follow Jesus at the cost of all else (as appropriate for their age), we can suggest to them they be baptised (immersed) in water, the Spirit and the body. What a joyful day that is!

4. Laying on of Hands: This is for the impartation of the Holy Spirit. When the Spirit of God is imparted, He manifests Himself in so many ways — healing, deliverance, power to minister. According to Acts 2:38, a passage that has been referred to as "the Peter package", Jesus always intended water baptism, Spirit baptism and baptism into the body to occur at the same time. When it didn't happen that way in the life of the early church, Jesus sent the apostle Paul to correct the foundations of the early Christians so that the church He was building would be built on a solid foundation. Acts 8:14-17, 10:44-48, and 19:1-9 are specific passages that describe the correcting of the foundations. We can demonstrate the power of this simple thing in our every-day life. We can lay hands on our younger children to receive a blessing from Jesus; we can teach them to lay hands on others and give a blessing; we can teach them about healing and deliverance through laying on of hands (as age appropriate).

5. Resurrection of the dead: 1 Corinthians 15 tells us about resurrection life. Jesus was the first to rise from the dead, as the first fruits, and we will follow Him in the Resurrection (verse 23). After this, Jesus will deliver the Kingdom to the Father. Regardless of what we believe about "end times", the Word of God is clear. Verse 24 tells us Jesus will *"deliver the kingdom to the Father"*. We ask ourselves "How can anyone deliver what is not yet established?" so the conclusion we end up with is that the Kingdom of God must already be established! Or at least in the process of being established. It is not something that will one day come (like the "pie in the sky when you die" teaching of heaven!). Another conclusion we arrive at is that this foundation is more about living *the new life* spoken of in Romans 6:7-14 and Galatians 2:19-20, *"walking in the Spirit"* rather than the flesh. There will come a time when we will inherit a resurrected body but, today, our old life has been crucified and we are alive in Him! We can demonstrate a life lived in the power of the resurrection until such as time when our children *"take up the cross"* for themselves (Luke 9:23).

6. Eternal judgement: This is another of those teachings that have been put off until after we reach heaven, but it is not so! We have already been judged and have passed from death into life (John 5:24). We have assurance of our salvation! Our assurance is rock solid — not because we have a strong will, or a strong conviction, but because the Word of God says so. That is where our strength lies.

Teaching Foundations

So how do we impart these teachings to our children? We give *"milk"* to babes and *"solid food"* to those who can digest it (1 Corinthians 3:2). We give them small amounts of teaching as life directs. When we need to correct behaviour in the younger years, it is reasonably easy to teach them about repentance. We can explain things to them, but we can also demonstrate, through actions. Walk in one direction and explain that their bad behaviour is taking them this way; down the road a bit (pointing with the hand) are all sorts of bad things, consequences and further issues; we have revelation (hitting our forehead with our hand) and we say "Oops, I just did something that displeases my earthly or heavenly Father"; turn around 180 degrees and begin walking in the opposite direction (pointing to forgiveness, good consequences and the fruit of the Spirit that lies in this direction) we say "I think I'll turn around and start walking back toward Jesus and His ways".

Asking for forgiveness is having *"faith toward God"*. Praying for our daily needs is having *"faith toward God"*. Reading Bible stories and singing songs to Jesus is building *"faith toward God"*. Living our lives by walking in the Spirit is a demonstration of faith to our children; it isn't just something they learn about at Church on Sundays or going to a Christian school. It is something they see demonstrated a home. It becomes part of their "normal" existence.

Reading the Bible as a family will impart so much to our children. Not only do they learn practical skills of reading and taking turns, they also learn spiritual skills to put into practice during the storms of life: facing pressures at school, such as exam time; facing social issues, such as the variability of friendships; facing emotional trauma, such as the increasing prevalence of bullying. This is a time to teach children to cry out to God for help, direction and deliverance.

When their faith is real and they can express their dependence on God as their Father, we can begin to teach them about baptisms. We may already have taught them through regular, family Bible readings. Being led by the Spirit, we will know when the time is right for them to be baptised. There is no age limit on baptism. I've known children as young as three be baptised and keep their faith all their lives; I've known adults who have been baptised but walked away from their faith when life gets tough. God knows.

Right Relationships

Family is the place to learn so many things that equip us for life in society. There is so much teamwork in a family that is functioning under the control of the Holy Spirit. The Bible includes mothers, fathers and children in its description of a family but in today's society, one or more of these functions is missing and other members take on the role of the missing person. Having right relationships is more an issue of the heart than a legal title or function.

Jesus, Christ the anointed Messiah, is *"head of His body, the church"* (Ephesians1:22, 5:23, Colossians 1:18). We need to be waking in the reality of this before we can teach it to our children. When we are demonstrating this is in our life, our children can see living examples of Bible truths. This, also, is a foundational teaching. It is part of the *"faith toward God"* foundation. Moving on from this, we can teach our children that Dad is the head of the home. Dad sits at the head of the table; he carves the meat at the table (either literally or figuratively). He has the overall management of affairs, even though it may be Mum who pays the bills. When decisions are required, Dad and Mum can talk about the issues together. God has given the wife to the husband to be *"a helper"* (Genesis 2:18), not to take over the family direction, nor to be a "doormat" upon which he treads. They are to be *"one flesh"*. When he has listened carefully and respectfully to her opinions and guidance, he then makes the final decision and she willingly submits to that *"as to the Lord"* (Colossians 3:18), knowing that God is directing her life through the decisions of her husband. I often think this is a harder exercise of *"faith toward to God"* than if I had decided only on my own interpretation of what I thought the Spirit was saying.

It goes without saying that we should pray and ask God's guidance for these issues we are facing. We place our trust and reliance on God for His direction in our lives. I can see God's sense of humour in this. Generally speaking, he has made man a little more reliant on the tangible indicators in life, whereas He has made the woman more open to the things of the spirit world. So, I can see God in His wisdom, saying "Hmmm. The woman has an advantage over the man so let's make her life a little bit more interesting: instead of getting her guidance directly from us, let's make it so that she has to rely on her husband, getting guidance for herself and the family from us". It sometimes takes a wee bit more faith to rely on God through the decisions of our husband!

We were facing a major issue in our life. Our business was losing money due to a widespread drought and we needed to close it and look for employment. I had suggested looking for employment in a particular town prior to the crisis point but it was not well received.

Eventually, though, my husband decided to look for work in the mining industry. He had to do a particular industry induction in order to make himself employable (at the age of 57). We decided (more him than me!) to spend the last $600 we had to pay for the induction course. My attitude was "If we die, we die". That was done and we began looking for work. A friend suggested a town five hours north of where we lived so we set out for this town, knowing we would have to relocate if he found work. While we were in this town, me husband read a regional newspaper that advertised jobs in another town a further six hours north. He decided we would go and look there, knowing that we were driving further and further away from our family. As were drove north, I was praying silently to my Father (after we had prayed together for the right direction) and I had a vision of a little gumnut resting on an upturned leaf as it was floating down a stream, being carried by the current. I knew that God was saying to me that I had no control over this process, whatsoever, but that He was the One carrying me. This was probably the clearest experience I've had of total submission to God through my husband.

So much is written on a wife's submission to her husband without the opposite, but equally important, directive to the husband to love and care for the wife, "*as Christ loved the church and gave Himself for her*" (Ephesians 5:25). This means that He is to guide his wife and family as he submits to Jesus, in the same way that Jesus submitted to His Father, God. She is to submit to her husband "*as unto the Lord*" (Ephesians 5:22). This means that she willingly places herself in the God-ordained place in the relationship, respecting her husband's leadership role.

She has her own sphere of authority. If she is a 'stay at home Mum' she is probably responsible for the housework, school transportation, paying bills, etc, just as determined jointly by both husband and wife. As she puts into practice these responsibilities, she may not do it as he would have done it, but he is not to be bitter toward her for not doing things his way. She is not a slave! There needs to be give and take; there needs to be communication between them; and, there needs to be a willingness to love and support each other.

There really is a partnership between them, and she should have the flexibility to make decisions within the framework set by the two of them. This is a display of our relationship to Jesus as the head of the church. He is the One building the church; He is the foundation and we are the "*living stones*" (1 Peter 2:5).

Children then fit into that framework, set by both parents, and demonstrate obedience. When they are young, as I've already said, their obedience is directed through external motivation but, eventually, God requires an obedience of the heart where their obedience is internally motivated. In Colossians 3:21, God is directing fathers to not **discourage** their children. It is the nature of a woman (generally speaking) to be soft and encouraging so God gives the direction to the fathers.

There is a definite hierarchy of decision making in the family: Jesus, fathers and mothers, then children. We need to teach our children that they follow a predefined order, or framework. As they grow older, we teach them the skills to make choices within set guidelines. Then we teach them to make those guidelines so that they are equipped to be a parent when it is their turn.

Romans 12:10 tells us to *"prefer one another"*. The family is the best place to practice putting the needs of others before our own.

> *Whatever you do, do it heartily as to the Lord and not to men.* **Colossians 3:23**

A SPECIAL OFFER

FOR CHURCHES AND SMALL STUDY GROUPS

Why not use the leader's guide to facilitate group study in this essential area of the Christian walk? Use it to encourage and support young disciples in their faith walk with Jesus.

To purchase a copy of the Leader's Guide, it can be found on the Author's page at Amazon, or go to:

http://www.elgembooks.com/LatestRelease

For some churches, the concept of how to walk in True discipleship maybe new. To introduce this important topic, speaking engagements and workshops can be arranged. To book a speaking engagement or workshop at your church go to:

www.elgembooks.com/Contact

To leave a **BOOK REVIEW**, you can also go to …

https://www.amazon.com.au/dp/0975767917/ref=cm_sw_em_r_mt_dp_Z3AtFbDFZATPH

OR

www.elgembooks .com

A PERSONAL REQUEST

For Individuals

Amazon review: Your reviews are like gold to authors! We literally cannot survive without them.

Redeem your FREE gift: To receive a FREE Personal Journal, join the Elgembooks Mailing List at http://eepurl.com/gIJ5_j. You can opt out at any time.

Extend the kingdom of God on earth: Beyond surviving as an author, there is another, even more important reason to write a review. It is extremely helpful to others as they search for information on this topic! When you provide a review, you will help others access this important information while on their journey of discipleship to Jesus! You will be a seed planted in the harvest, sent out to do the work of the Master! Your simple review could be the difference between someone just surviving as a mother and one that is empowered to transform children's lives as disciples. You will touch others with "grace and apostleship" (Romans 1:5).

My thanks: I wish to communicate to you how grateful I am! I began this journey thinking "Who do I think I am to be writing a book with such an important topic?" but I have also found freedom to be creative, realizing that I was "born for such a time as this" (Esther 4:14). By using my gifts, others will see the "good works" and "glorify my father which is in heaven" (Matthew 5:16).

To God be the glory...
Lexia G Mackin

www.ingramcontent.com/pod-product-compliance
Lightning Source LLC
Chambersburg PA
CBHW052028290426
44112CB00014B/2427